Designing and Pattern Cutting for Children's Clothes

Designing and Pattern Cutting
for Children's Clothes

Peter Morgan

B. T. Batsford Limited
London

© Peter Morgan 1973

ISBN 0 7134 2712 4

First published 1973
Reprinted 1977

Filmset by Servis Filmsetting Ltd, Manchester
Printed in Great Britain by
Wm Clowes Ltd, Beccles, Suffolk
for the publishers B. T. Batsford Limited
4 Fitzhardinge Street
London W1H 0AH

Contents

Acknowledgement

The author wishes to thank the following for their kind assistance in the preparation of this book: Ann Harding, pattern cutting lecturer at the Polytechnic, Newcastle upon Tyne, who checked over the completed manuscript, and Wilfred Rodwell, F.C.I., whose report, 'Towards Metric Sizing' was invaluable.

Section 1 *Metrication, measuring and equipment*

METRICATION

It has been apparent for many years that the multiplicity of sizes together with the various criteria used to establish these sizes by different manufacturers has caused a considerable amount of confusion to both the retailer and consumer in the field of children's wear. It is possible to obtain children's clothing where the size indication is based upon the chest measurement, actual or nominal length of a garment, height of a child and even the least reliable of all, age. These variations cause endless difficulties to the retailer trying to rationalize his stock as well as making it almost impossible to shop for a child without the child being present.

This situation could probably have been prolonged indefinitely had it not been necessary for the clothing trade to take a comprehensive look at its own industry and the problems which could be caused by the legal requirements of metrication in the mid-1970s.

A committee was formed from the professional interests of the trade to represent all sides of industry from yarn and cloth manufacturers, garment makers, component suppliers and retailers through to the consumer, as well as the British Standards Institution. Their brief was basically to investigate and recommend changes which would have to be implemented throughout every aspect of the clothing industry to comply with the forthcoming metrication. The committee was concerned with technical details such as new standards for weights and widths of cloth, sewing thread specifications, needle sizes, suitable making-up allowances on garments, labelling, and so on, as well as the new metric sizing standards which would radically affect men's, women's, and children's clothing.

For children's sizing, the experiences of continental countries could be drawn upon. For many years they have used a system of sizing which takes the total height of a child as a basic measurement around which other measurements could be tabulated. It is interesting to note that as long ago as 1953, at a Garment Sizing Conference in this country, a committee was formed which subsequently concluded that height was the most reliable indication of a child's size. Unfortunately, it was never implemented by the children's wear manufacturers. The continental method, called the 'Centilong System', originated in Sweden in the late 1950s and has been adopted by other important continental countries such as France, Italy, Germany, Holland and Switzerland, where it has been readily accepted by the manufacturer, retailer, and the consumer. Experience seems to prove that it is the most universally accurate system of sizing children's clothes.

However, as with any sizing system which attempts to cover all children, it fits the 'average' child most successfully. About 75% of any size grouping is of an approximately average fit, but because manufacturers in most European countries do not make sub-sizes, those children who are not quite average will perhaps have some difficulty in obtaining a satisfactory garment.

Although in principle, height has been agreed as the main criteria for establishing the 'Centilong System', local variations have taken place. The major deviation has been in the non-establishment of a common size interval. Sweden and Italy have a size interval of 5 cm while most other European countries have an interval of 6 cm. For this country, the British Standards Institution's recommendation for the size interval is 6 cm. Even among countries which have a 6 cm size interval there have been slight differences. This is because they have started from different points on the height scale. In France, for example, the size chart reads 102, 108, 114, 120, and so forth, while in Holland, Germany and the United Kingdom the nearest equivalent is 104, 110, 116, 122. Although these divergences might prove to some people that it is impossible to rationalize children's sizing on a European basis, the important point is that various European countries have all reached one same conclusion, that height is the most important single factor by which children's sizing methods can be accurately assessed.

As for infants and toddlers, most parents are more aware of their weight rather than their height at this stage in their development. Therefore, the weight, in kilogrammes, is also given in the British Standards Size Chart. Infants and toddlers are outside the scope of this book, but further, more detailed information can be found in the British Standards Institute's publication, B.S. 3728.

MEASURING A CHILD

The measurements in the British Standards Chart are body measurements with no tolerance allowed. Diagrams 1a and 1b show the positions on the body from where they are taken and the numbers also relate to the sequence in the British Standards Chart. When measuring children, make sure that they are standing perfectly straight, and in a natural relaxed position. Not all of the measurements follow the contours of the body.

2 Height the total height taken vertically from the highest point.

4 Chest taken round the body over the fullest part of the chest.

5 Waist the true waist.

6 Hip the true hip. Measurement 15 can be used as a guideline to establish the depth of the hip.

7 Across Back a line over the shoulder blades from points approximately midway between the top and bottom of the armhole.

8 Armscye Girth a line around the arm at the point where it joins the body.

9 Neck Base taken around the neck where it sits on the shoulders.

10 Shoulder from the base of the neck at the side to the top of the shoulder.

11 Upper Arm measured around the bicep.

12 Thigh Girth measured around the widest part of the thigh.

13 Scye Depth measured from the nape of the neck to an imaginary point directly below it and level with the bottom of the arm where it joins the body.

14 Neck to Waist taken from the nape of the neck following the body contour to the centre back of the waist.

15 Waist to Hip the distance from the waist at the side to the most prominent part of the hip.

16 Cervical Height the height taken vertically from the nape of the neck to the ground.

17 Cervical to Knee the measurement taken vertically from the nape of the neck to a point level with the back of the knee.

18 Body Rise when a child is sitting on a horizontal surface, the measurement taken vertically from the waist to the horizontal surface.

19 Sideseam the measurement taken vertically from the side waist to the ground.

20 Vertical Trunk from the centre of the right shoulder down the back and under the crotch, returning over the stomach and chest to the centre of the right shoulder.

21 Crotch Length from the centre back waist under the crotch to the centre front waist.

22 Shoulder and Arm a combined measurement from the neck base at the shoulder to the wrist taken over a relaxed bent arm.

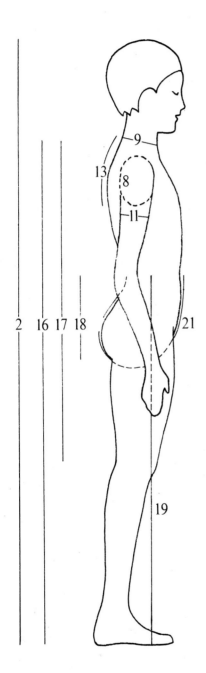

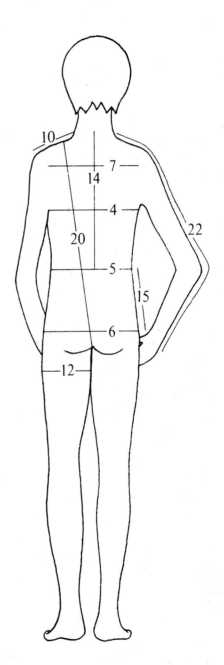

1a   Measuring a child   1b

EQUIPMENT

Apart from the tracing wheel and balance notchers, the equipment is non-specialized and easily obtainable from most stationers, art suppliers or department stores. As so little is needed, it is worthwhile having the best quality available.

Tracing wheel
A small spiked wheel about two centimetres in diameter on the end of a handle. It is used for transferring pattern lines by pricking holes through the top pattern piece to paper or card underneath.

Balance notcher
A small punch which cuts out a U-shaped balance mark on the pattern wherever necessary. A balance mark is a reference point on a pattern which enables the pattern pieces and subsequently the garment sections to be put together at the correct point.

Set square
When constructing a block or pattern, this is essential for establishing absolutely accurate right angles. It should be fairly rigid, in a transparent plastic with clearly defined measurements in centimetres. Wooden set squares often warp and become inaccurate, and for this reason should not be used.

Metre rule
Accurately marked in centimetres, and available in wood or metal, although metal is preferable. It is needed for establishing long straight lines.

French curve
A clear plastic shape which contains various curved edges rather than straight lines. It is used for obtaining curved shapes on a pattern, such as a neck or arm scye.

Tape measure
Some stretch and lose their markings after constant use, so a good one is essential. There are excellent glass fibre ones available, marked in centimetres.

Scissors
These should be comfortable to handle. About twenty centimetres is a reasonable length. Although not essential, it is very useful to have one pair for paper and heavier, weighted scissors for card.

Paper
This must be large enough for the size of the pattern which is being drafted. As pattern lines are sometimes drawn many times before they are correct, it is best to choose a paper with a rigid surface which will not disintegrate too easily with constant rubbings out. A paper which is not quite opaque is useful as lines can be traced through if necessary. Special pattern paper, plain or scaled, can be bought.

Card
A firm card is used in the trade for basic blocks, and although this is normally bought in rolls, large sheets of card, provided they are firm enough, will be sufficient.

Pencils
Although it seems elementary to mention pencils, it is important to use a hard pencil, 4H or more, and keep it sharpened. Anything much softer will lead to inaccurate work by causing lines to become blurred and smudged.

Felt tip pens
Brilliant clear colours are available, and these are very good for marking any information on the block or pattern such as size, grain lines, cutting instructions and so on.

Weights
As it is necessary to hold large pattern pieces steady, small weights of any description are useful.

Rubber
A soft type which will not score the paper.

Sellotape (Scotch Tape) and Dressmaking pins
Both are useful for temporarily joining pattern
pieces together. As *Sellotape* shrinks and causes
wrinkles in paper, it is not advisable to use it as a
permanent measure because the pattern will
become distorted and inaccurate.

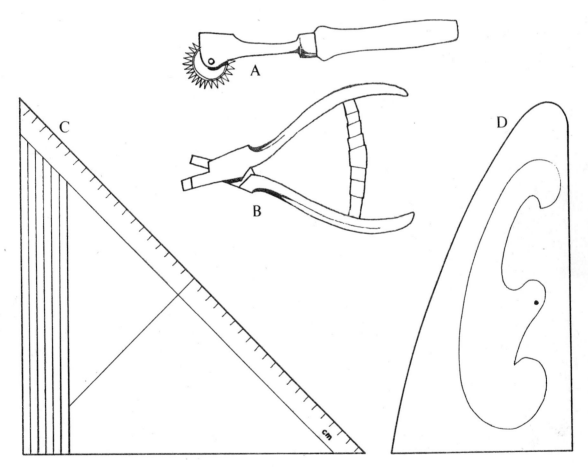

2 Equipment. *a* tracing wheel, *b* balance notcher,
   c set square, *d* french curve

		BOYS/GIRLS				GIRLS					
I	APPROX. AGE	2	3	4	5	6	7	8	9	10	11
2	HEIGHT ✓	92	98	104	110	116	122	128	134	140	146
3	WEIGHT	ONLY APPLICABLE TO INFANT SIZES									
4	CHEST ✓	53	55	57	59	61	63	66	69	72	76
5	WAIST ✓	52	53	54	55	57	58	59	61	62	63
6	HIP ✓	56·5	59	61	63·5	66	68	71·5	75	78·5	83
7	CROSSBACK	22	22·5	23	24	25	26	27	28	29	30
8	ARMSCYE GIRTH	24	25	26	27	28	29	30	31	32	33·5
9	NECK BASE	25	26	26·5	27·5	28	29	30	31	32	33
10	SHOULDER	7·3	7·5	8	8·3	8·5	9	9·3	9·5	9·8	10
11	UPPER ARM	16	16·5	17	17·5	18	18·5	19	20	20·5	21·5
12	THIGH GIRTH	31	32	33	35	37	39	41	43	45	47
13	SCYE DEPTH	10·5	11	12	12·5	13·5	14	15	15·5	16·5	17
14	NECK—WAIST	22	23	24	25·5	27	28	29·5	30·5	32	33·5
15	WAIST—HIP	10·5	11	12	12·5	13·5	14	15	15·5	16·5	17
16	CERVICAL HEIGHT	76	81·5	87	92	98	103	109	114	119	125
17	CERVICAL TO KNEE	51	54	57	61	65	69	72	76	80	84
18	BODY RISE	17	18	19	20	21	22	23	24	25·5	26·5
19	SIDESEAM	56	60	64	68	72	77	81	85	89	93
20	VERTICAL TRUNK	90	94	99	103	107	112	116	121	127	134
21	CROTCH LENGTH	45	47	49	51	53	55	57	60	63	66
22	SHOULDER AND ARM	36·5	39	42	45	48	51	54	57	60	63

All the measurements are in centimetres.

Section 2   Construction of the basic blocks

A basic block is a simplified pattern, usually made of card, which is used as a foundation for the construction of other patterns. For ease of use and manipulation no unnecessary fullness is added. It is cut net, that is, there are no seam allowances.

One point which must be emphasized is that although the term, basic block, tends to indicate that it is something which is quite final and which can only be made one way, this is in fact not so. Fashion alters constantly from year to year, generally as part of a cyclical pattern, and as part of this movement it is usual for basic blocks to change as well. They do not alter radically, but subtle changes do take place in the silhouette. The cut and shape of the armscye might vary to take a differently fitting sleeve, or the slope of the shoulders could change to allow for padding or a wide-shouldered effect. In women's blocks, the bust dart controlling the fullness can be under the bust, an underarm dart or a shoulder dart. These variations can be in different basic blocks and none of them are necessarily incorrect. It simply means that given a set of measurements, different pattern drafters, though seeking the same ends, will use different means of achieving them.

The wide variation of fit in children's clothes is not so much due to rapid alteration in fashion, but to the different tolerances made by manufacturers to allow for the constant change in shape and size of a continuously growing child. While it is necessary to have a sufficient amount of tolerance, or ease, in a child's block to allow for growth and movement, it is important that it fits and hangs correctly. If it ever appears necessary to have extra allowances, these can always be worked into the style and design of a garment in the form of pleats and gathers while the basic fit remains unaltered.

Studying the British Standards Chart on page 12, it is apparent that unlike adult size charts there is not always a regular increase between sizes. This is because a child, although growing continually in height and width, is not developing every part of its body at a constant rate. A child will often grow in height very rapidly, and then appear to remain static while laterally the rest of his body catches up. However, an average child grows about a size a year. This means a chest increase of 2 cm every year for 2 to 7-year-olds and about 3 cms for 7 to 11-year-old children. Although the height increase per year and size is about 6 cm, the important measurement affecting block construction is that of the back neck to waist. This is 1–1·5 cm per size. The cervical to knee measurement, which is a great help with proportion when drafting patterns from basic blocks, is 3–4 cm depending upon the size.

It is relatively simple to construct the basic blocks by following the drafting instructions, in conjunction with the diagrams, in a logical manner. The most difficult part is the establishment of good shapes, such as the armhole or crotch curves. Although the French curve will help a great deal, if used properly, there is no mechanical substitute for practice and a trained eye. Only through trial and error will it be possible to distinguish between a line which is satisfactorily balanced and one which is not truly acceptable.

Before constructing any block, one noteworthy point is that although the darts in the illustrations appear to be cut out, this is only done for clarification of the diagrams. When drafting, do not cut the dart away because this will weaken the block and cause it to tear easily at the dart points. If needed, the apex of any dart can be cut out, leaving the bottom part intact.

Always ensure that any information relative to a block is fully noted upon it, such as size, balance marks, ease allowances and any particular measurement that might be needed.

THE BASIC BODICE BLOCK

A basic bodice block is not a full block. It represents half of the back and half of the front and in this construction both halves are drafted together.

A tolerance of 8 cm is allowed on the chest, 6 cm round the waist, and approximately 3 cm around the armscye for a fitted sleeve. Small children tend to have rather large stomachs and this has been allowed for in the three smallest sizes. There are no waist darts to suppress any shaping because the fullness is needed to compensate for the extra bulk found in this area of small children. Diagram 3 illustrates the waist shaping of sizes 92, 98 and 104.

It is well known that the onset of puberty is earlier in successive generations. For this reason it is quite likely that the two larger-sized blocks will not always give a satisfactory fit. There is no allowance for the development and shape of an early adolescent figure: they are designed to fit children who still have typical children's figures. Before constructing the block make sure that the card or pattern paper is sufficiently large enough for the whole draft to be completed. It should be approximately 5 or 6 cm longer in depth and width than the measurements A–B and A–C of the size being constructed.

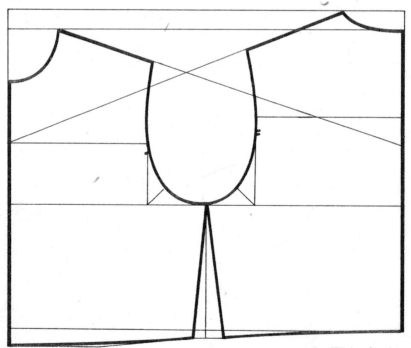

3   Waist shaping, sizes 92, 98, 104

SIZE	92	98	104	110	116	122	128	134	140	146	
A–B	23·5	24·5	25·5	27	28·5	29·5	31	32	33·5	35	nape to waist + _back neck depth_
A–C	30·5	31·5	32·5	33·5	34·5	35·5	37	38·5	40	42	½ chest + tolerance

includes 4·0 4·0 4·0 4·0 4·0 4·0 4·0 4·0 4·0 4·0   *tolerance*

Square down from C approximately 5–6 cm
longer than A–B, to establish the centre front line.

	92	98	104	110	116	122	128	134	140	146	
A–D	1·5	1·5	1·5	1·5	1·5	1·5	1·5	1·5	1·5	1·5	_back neck depth_
B–E	8·5	9·2	9·9	10·6	11·4	12	12·8	13·5	14·7	15·5	

F midway between D–E.
Square D–G, E–H, B, to centre front line.

	92	98	104	110	116	122	128	134	140	146	
F–I	11·5	11·8	12	12·5	13	13·5	14	14·5	15	15·5	½ cross back + tolerance

includes ·5 ·55 ·5 ·5 ·5 ·5 ·5 ·5 ·5 ·5   *tolerance*

Square I–J to chest line.

	92	98	104	110	116	122	128	134	140	146	
G–K	4·8	5·0	5·2	5·4	5·6	5·8	6·0	6·2	6·4	6·6	_front neck depth_

L midway between K–H.

	92	98	104	110	116	122	128	134	140	146	
K–M	19·7	20·4	21·1	22·3	23·5	24·2	25·4	26·1	27·3	28·5	_front neck/waist_
L–N	11	11·3	11·5	12	12·5	13	13·5	14	14·5	15	½ cross front + tolerance

Square N–O to chest line.

	92	98	104	110	116	122	128	134	140	146	
E–P	15	15·5	16	16·5	16·9	17·4	18·1	18·9	19·6	20·5	½ back chest width

Square P–Q.

	92	98	104	110	116	122	128	134	140	146	
P–Q	9·0	9·7	10·4	11·1	11·8	12·5	13·3	14	15·2	16	_side seam length_

G–R same as G–K.

	92	98	104	110	116	122	128	134	140	146	
S–A	4·6	4·8	5·0	5·2	5·4	5·6	5·8	6·0	6·2	6·4	

Connect R to a point 2·5 cm below F.
Connect S–L.

SIZE	92	98	104	110	116	122	128	134	140	146	
S–T	7·8	8·0	8·5	8·8	9·0	9·5	9·8	10	10·3	10·5	*back shoulder+ tolerance*
R–U	7·3	7·5	8·0	8·3	8·5	9·0	9·3	9·5	9·8	10	*front shoulder*
O–O1	1·5	1·5	1·5	1·8	1·8	1·8	2·0	2·0	2·2	2·2	*O–O1 bisects the angle NOP*
J–J1	2·0	2·0	2·0	2·3	2·3	2·3	2·5	2·5	2·7	2·7	*J–J1 bisects the angle IJP*

Connect points U, N, O1, P, J1, I and T with a good curve to form the armscye shape.

Square out from Q to Q1 and Q2.

	92	98	104	110	116	122	128	134	140	146	
Q–Q1	0·8	1·1	1·2	0·4	0·4	0·6	0·5	0·8	0·8	1·0	*side seam shaping*
Q–Q2	0·9	1·1	1·3	0·7	0·7	1·0	0·9	1·1	1·1	1·5	*side seam shaping*
B–V	7·0	7·0	7·5	7·5	7·5	8·0	8·0	8·5	8·5	9·0	

Square V–W.

	92	98	104	110	116	122	128	134	140	146	
V–W				10	10·5	11	11·5	12	12·5	13	*height of back dart*
V–V1				0·5	0·5	0·5	0·7	0·7	1·0	1·2	*width of back dart*
V–V2				0·5	0·5	0·5	0·8	0·8	1·0	1·3	

Connect B–V1–W–V2–Q2.

	92	98	104	110	116	122	128	134	140	146	
M–X	7·0	7·0	7·5	7·5	7·5	8·0	8·0	8·5	8·5	9·0	

Square X–Y.

	92	98	104	110	116	122	128	134	140	146	
X–Y				11·5	12	12·5	13	13·5	14	14·5	*height of front dart*
X–X1				0·5	0·5	0·5	0·7	0·7	1·0	1·2	*width of front dart*
X–X2				0·5	0·5	0·5	0·8	0·8	1·0	1·3	

Connect M–X2–Y–X1–Q1.

For waist shaping on sizes 92, 98 and 104, connect M–Q1 and B–Q2 with good curves using the points M–X–Q1 and B–V–Q2 as guide lines. Make the front curve slightly above X and the back curve below V. (See diagram 3.)

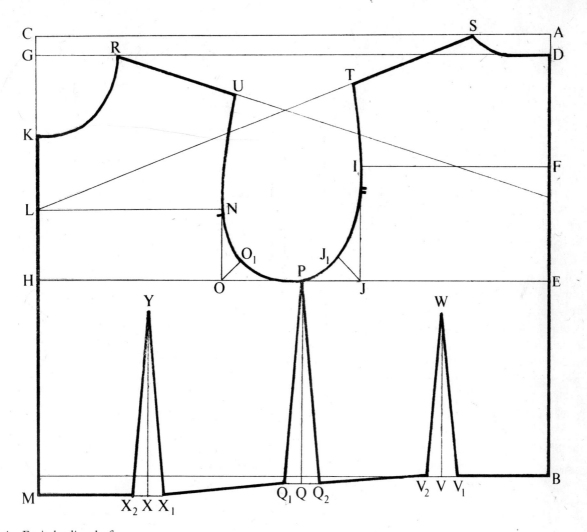

4   Basic bodice draft

Children's clothes are not normally as intricately shaped and cut as adult clothes and apart from the more shaped sleeve in a coat or jacket this applies to the cut of children's sleeves as well. This has been taken into account in the draft of this particular basic sleeve block which is quite straight. It has no shaping at the seam edge and is far more useful as a child's basic block than many of the adult basic sleeve blocks. These normally have elbow darts which help to control the fullness and reduce the width at the wrist enabling a closer fit to be obtained. Less fitted sleeves are used for children so there is no need to draft a fitted one. For most patterns, the dart would have to be removed before the block could be used in its most basic form. The arm bends at the elbow when held in a relaxed position and the back of the arm is therefore longer than the front. To allow for this the block is shaped at the wrist level, being deeper at the back of the sleeve and cut away at the front. It is not an exaggerated line, but it does give a better balanced look to the hang of the sleeve. This shaping should be kept whenever the block is used for pattern making. The block has 4 cm tolerance around the bicep, and 2 cm ease over the sleevehead in the smaller sizes, rising to 3·5 cm ease in the larger sizes. In any sleeve, the area above line C_1–C_2 in diagram 5 is known as the sleevehead and the topmost part of this, either side of point A, is known as the crown of the sleeve.

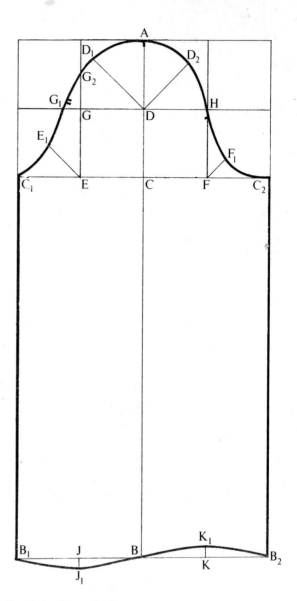

5 Basic sleeve draft

Draft of the sleeve block   Diagram 5
Construct a rectangle to the following measurements:

SIZE	92	98	104	110	116	122	128	134	140	146	
WIDTH	20	20·5	21	21·5	22	22·5	23	24	24·5	25·5	*bicep + tolerance*
LENGTH	32	33·5	35·5	37·5	39·8	41·8	44·3	46·8	49·5	52	*posterior sleeve length + tolerance*

18

Halve the rectangle vertically and on this line mark the following points. A is the top of the rectangle.

D midway between A–C.
Square from B to establish points B1–B2.

SIZE	92	98	104	110	116	122	128	134	140	146	
A–B	31·5	33	35	37	39	41	43·5	46	48·5	51	outside sleeve length
A–C	9·5	9·8	10	10·5	11	11·5	12	12·5	12·8	13·5	depth of sleeve crown

Square from C to establish points C1–C2.
Square from D to the edges of the rectangle.
E midway between C–C1.
F midway between C–C2.

From points E and F construct vertical lines which cross the lines squared out from D, at points G and H, and meet the top edge of the rectangle.

D–D1	4·9	5·1	5·3	5·5	5·8	6·1	6·4	6·6	6·7	7·1	D–D1 bisects the angle ADG
D–D2	4·4	4·6	4·9	5·1	5·3	5·4	5·6	5·7	6·0	6·4	D–D2 bisects the angle ADH
E–E1	3·2	3·2	3·3	3·5	3·7	3·9	4·0	4·1	4·3	4·4	E–E1 bisects the angle GEC1
F–F1	2·0	2·1	2·3	2·4	2·5	2·5	2·6	2·6	2·7	2·8	F–F1 bisects the angle HFC2
G–G1	0·8	0·9	1·0	1·1	1·2	1·3	1·4	1·5	1·6	1·7	
G–G2	1·6	1·8	2·0	2·2	2·4	2·6	2·8	3·0	3·2	3·4	

Join points C1–E1–G1–G2–D1–A–D2–H–F1–C2 with a good curve to form the shape of the sleevehead.

J midway between B–B1.
K midway between B–B2.

J–J1	0·5	0·5	0·5	0·5	0·8	0·8	0·8	0·8	1·0	1·0	J–J1 is at right angles to B–B1
K–K1	0·5	0·5	0·5	0·5	0·8	0·8	0·8	0·8	1·0	1·0	K–K1 is at right angles to B–B2

Join points B1–J1–B–K1–B2 with a good curved line to establish the wrist shaping. The lefthand side of the block is the back of the sleeve.

Insertion of sleeve and bodice balance marks
Diagram 6

For a sleeve to hang correctly in an armhole, it must have the correct balance marks. A balance mark is a reference point drafted into blocks or patterns so that when corresponding points are placed together, the fit is always correct. When transferred from the pattern to a garment it enables the garment sections to be put together properly so that the cloth is not distorted in any way.

Place the underarm points of the front bodice block and the front of the sleeve block together and pivot the sleeve so that as much of the two edges coincide as possible. At the point where the edges diverge pivot again so that the edges coincide and where they diverge repeat the

process until a point about halfway along the bodice block has been reached. Mark this point on both the bodice and sleeve blocks to establish the front balance mark. Continue to pivot the sleeve until the shoulder point has been reached and mark this on the sleeve block.

Repeat the whole process for the back bodice and sleeve, but make two balance marks about 0·5 cm apart. This will always distinguish the back from the front of the sleevehead and any ease for the sleeve crown should be distributed between these two balance marks. Continue to pivot until the shoulder point has been reached. Make a balance mark midway between the two points on the crown of the sleeve which were established from the shoulder points. This balance mark will always coincide with the shoulder seam.

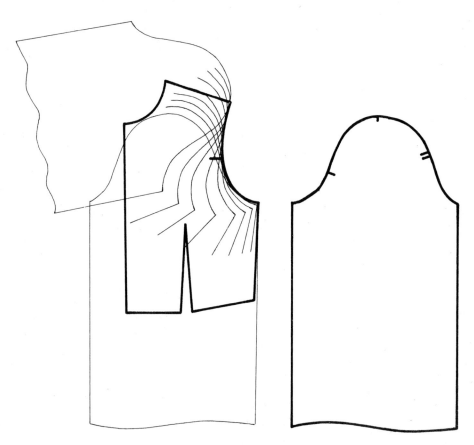

6   Positioning of balance marks

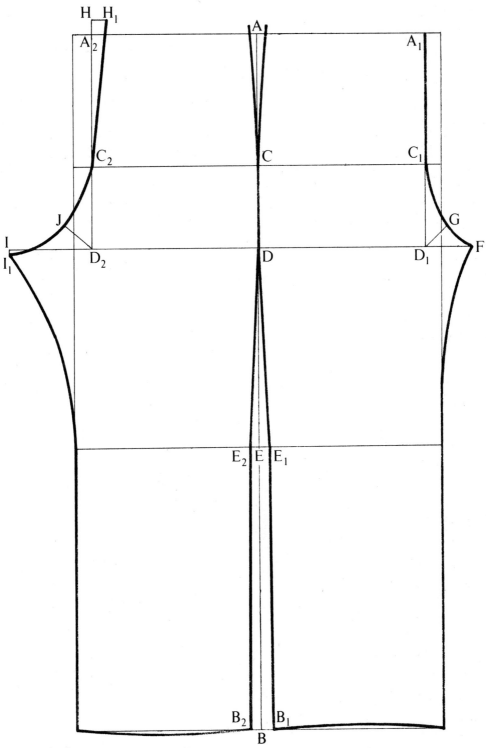

7 Basic trouser draft

As a child grows up, the waist-hip interval becomes more pronounced, from 4·5 cm in size 92 to 20 cm in size 146. This makes it impossible to give one set of drafting instructions which would apply accurately to each size. The construction of the block varies slightly in some details for the smaller and larger sizes.

The waist-hip difference is so small in size 92 that the shaping need only be taken from the sideseams. In size 98 a back dart is necessary as well as the shaping in the sideseam. For the two largest sizes, the waist definition has been established by two darts. Although it could be contained quite easily in one large dart, the shape would not be as subtle and the fit would not be as satisfactory as that achieved when two darts are used. On all other sizes, the waist suppression has been distributed through the sideseam and the back and front darts.

The waist of the basic block is the natural waist and any variation from this would be carried out in the subsequent pattern making.

The tolerance for the hip is 6 cm and around the waist 4 cm. This allows for growth without making any size appear too large and shapeless.

The draft of the leg section gives a basic straight silhouette.

Draft of the trouser block   Diagram 7
Construct a rectangle to the given measurements, but first note the following point. As the rectangle is only a framework and some of the construction lines extend beyond it, an allowance of at least 10 cm all round must be made to ensure that the card is large enough to contain the final draft.

SIZE	92	98	104	110	116	122	128	134	140	146	
WIDTH	34·2	35·5	36·5	37·7	39	40	41·7	43·5	45·2	47·5	
LENGTH	54	58	62	66	70	74	78	82	86	90	

Halve the rectangle vertically with the line A–B and mark the following points on it.

13·2

	92	98	104	110	116	122	128	134	140	146	
A–C	10·5	11	12	12·5	13·5	14	15	15·5	16·5	17	*depth of waist to hip*
A–D	18	19	20	(21)	22	23	24·5	25·5	27	28	*body rise+ tolerance*

E midway between C–B and is the knee level.

From points C and E square out to the edges of the rectangle.

Extend line D at least 10 cm beyond the rectangle each side.

Front trouser crotch shaping

	92	98	104	110	116	122	128	134	140	146	
A–A1	16·1	16·7	17·2	17·8	18·5	19	19·8	20·7	21·6	22·7	

C–C1 equals A–A1.
D–D1 equals A–A1.
Join A1–C1–D1.

SIZE	92	98	104	110	116	122	128	134	140	146	
D1–F	3·6	3·8	4·0	4·2	4·4	4·6	4·8	5·0	5·2	5·4	
D1–G	2·0	2·2	2·4	2·6	2·8	3·0	3·2	3·4	3·5	3·6	D1–G bisects the angle C1, D1, F

Connect C1–G–F with a good line to form the front crotch shaping.

Back trouser crotch shaping

A–A2	15·1	15·8	16·3	16·9	17·5	18	18·9	19·8	20·6	21·8	

C–C2 equals A–A2.
D–D2 equals A–A2.
Join D2–C2–A2 extending the line beyond A2 to point H.

A2–H	1·0	1·1	1·2	1·3	1·4	1·5	1·6	1·7	1·8	1·9	
D2–I	7·1	7·3	7·5	7·7	7·9	8·1	8·3	8·5	8·9	9·1	
D2–J	3·3	3·5	3·7	3·8	3·9	4·1	4·3	4·5	4·7	4·9	D2–J bisects the angle C2, D2, I
H–H1	1·3	1·5	1·5	1·7	1·4	1·5	1·8	2·1	2·3	2·6	waist suppression at back seam

I1 0·5 cm below I on all sizes.
Connect points H1–C2–J–I1 with a good curve to form the crotch shape.

Leg section, all sizes
E–E1, E–E2, B–B1, B–B2 are equal.

E–E1	0·5	0·6	0·7	0·8	0·9	1·0	1·1	1·2	1·3	1·4	

Connect C–D–E1–B1 to establish the front sideseam.

Connect C–D–E2–B2 to establish the back sideseam.

Connect F and I1 to the main construction lines above the knee line as shown in diagram 7 to complete the inside seam shape.

Curve the back hemline 0·5 cm below the baseline and the front hemline 0·5 cm above the baseline for a shaped hem.

Waist shaping   Diagram 8   Front, sizes 92–146.
Back, sizes 92–134

SIZE	92	98	104	110	116	122	128	134	140	146	
A1–O	7·8	8·0	8·3	8·5	8·8	9·1	9·4	9·9	10·2	10·6	

Square O–P.

O–P			8·5	9·0	9·5	10	10·5	11	11·5	12	*depth of front dart*
O–O1			0·5	0·5	0·5	0·5	0·8	0·8	0·8	1·0	*width of front dart*
O–O2			0·5	0·5	0·5	0·5	0·7	0·7	0·7	1·0	

Extend line A to Q and square to Q1 and Q2.

A–Q	0·3	0·4	0·4	0·4	0·5	0·5	0·5	0·5	0·6	0·6	
Q–Q1	0·5	0·5	0·5	0·5	0·7	1·0	1·0	1·0	1·2	1·2	*sideseam shaping*
Q–Q2	0·5	0·5	0·5	0·5	0·8	1·0	1·0	1·0	1·3	1·3	

Sizes 92–98
Connect A1–O–Q1–C to form the front trouser shaping. There is no front dart.

Sizes 104–146
Connect A1–O2–P–O1–Q1–C to form the waist shaping for these sizes.

Back: Size 92
Connect H1–Q2. There is no back dart.

Sizes 98–134
Connect H1–Q2. Midway on this line mark point R and square R–S.

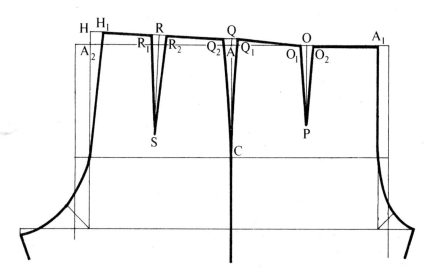

8   Waist shaping, front sizes 92–146, back
sizes 92–134

SIZE	98	104	110	116	122	128	134	
R–S	10·5	11	11·5	12	12·5	13	13·5	*length of back dart*
R–R1	0·8	0·5	0·8	0·8	0·8	1·0	1·3	*width of back dart*
R–R2	0·7	0·5	0·7	0·7	0·7	1·0	1·2	

Connect H1–R1–S–R2–Q2–C to form the back trouser waist shaping.

SIZE	140	146
Q2–R	5·0	5·5
Q2–T	10	11
R–S	14	14·5
T–U	14·5	15·0
R–R1	0·8	1·0
R–R2	0·7	1·0
T–T1	0·8	1·0
T–T2	0·7	1·0

Sizes 140–146   Diagram 9
Connect H1–Q2. On this line measure Q2–R and Q2–T.

Square R–S and T–U.

Connect H1–T1–U–T2–R1–S–R2–Q2–C to form the back darts for the waist shaping.
On all sizes the lines Q1–C and Q2–C should be very slightly curved as in diagram 8 to allow for the contour of the hip.

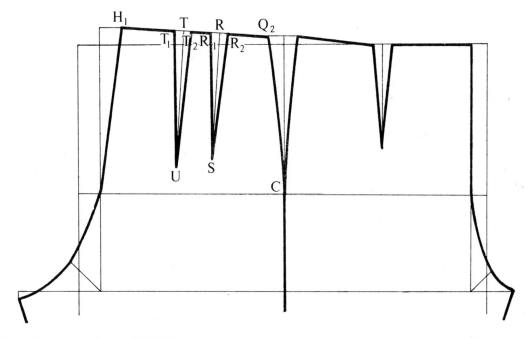

9   Waist shaping, back sizes 140–146

This block is useful as the basis for other styles rather than for use on its own. The difference between the waist and hip measurements is so slight, particularly in small children, that a skirt can be impractical because it never stays in place. With older children the waist-hip difference is greater so a skirt can remain firmly in position.

The waist ease for sizes 92–110 is 6 cm, allowing the block to be used with the bodice block. For sizes 116–146 it is 4 .cm. The ease on the hip is 6 cm for all sizes. The length of the block, measurement A–B, is taken from the back waist to the knee. For practical purposes, this would appear to be too long for a child, because it is a body measurement and not an arbitrary one, but nevertheless it is a good reference point. The length can be adjusted by measuring up from the hem and cutting off the unwanted amount. The skirt is slightly flared.

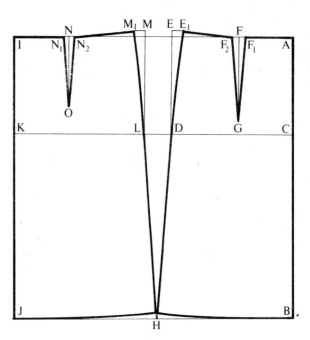

10   Basic skirt draft, sizes 92–134

Draft of the basic skirt
Sizes 92–134   Diagram 10
Construct a rectangle to the following width and length with point B in the bottom right hand corner.

SIZE	92	98	104	110	116	122	128	134	140	146	
WIDTH	35·2	36·5	37·5	38·7	40	41	42·8	44·5	46·3	48·5	
LENGTH	30	32	34	36	39	42	44	47	50	52	
A–B	29	31	33	35	38	40	42	45	48	50	*waist to knee*

Square A–I on the centre front line.

A–C	10·5	11	12	12·5	13·5	14	15	15·5	16·5	17	*waist to hip*

Square C–K.

B–H	17·1	17·8	18·3	18·9	19·5	20	20·9	21·8	22·6	23·8	
C–D	15·1	15·8	16·3	16·9	17·5	18	18·9	19·8	20·6	21·8	$\frac{1}{2}$ *back hip plus ease*

Square D–E.

SIZE	92	98	104	110	116	122	128	134	140	146	
D–E	11	11·5	12·6	13·1	14·2	14·7	15·8	16·3	17·4	17·9	

Square E–E1.

	92	98	104	110	116	122	128	134	140	146	
E–E1	1·3	1·9	1·7	2·1	1·5	1·9	1·9	2·3	1·7	1·5	
A–F	7·0	7·0	7·5	7·5	7·5·	8·0	8·0	8·5	6·0	6·5	

Sizes 92–110
Connect A–F–E1 to complete the waist.
    Square F–G.

					116	122	128	134	140	146	
F–G					12	12·5	13	13·5	14	14·5	*depth of back dart*
F–F1					0·7	0·7	1·0	1·0	1·0	1·5	*width of back dart*
F–F2					0·8	0·8	1·0	1·0	1·0	1·5	

Sizes 116–134
Connect A–F1–G–F2–E1 to complete the waist.

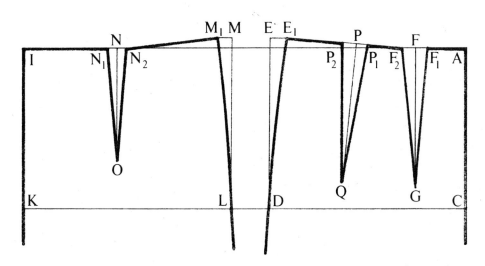

11   Back waist shaping, sizes 140–146

Back waist sizes 140–146   Diagram 11

SIZE	140	146	
F2–P	5·0	5·5	
P–Q	14	14·5	*depth of back dart*
P–P1	1·0	1·5	*width of back dart*
P–P2	1·0	1·5	

Connect F2–E1.
Mark off F2–P and square P–Q.

Sizes 140–146
Connect A–F1–G–F2–P1–Q–P2–E1 to complete
the waist. Just above H square a line to meet a
point midway on line B–H. Connect H–D–E1 to
complete the sideseam slightly curving the line
D–E1 for the contour of the hip.

Front skirt
  I–J equals A–B.
  I–K equals A–C.

SIZE	92	98	104	110	116	122	128	134	140	146	
K–L	16·1	16·7	17·2	17·8	18·5	19	19·8	20·7	21·6	22·7	½ *front hip plus ease*

Square L–M.

L–M	11	11·5	12·6	13·1	14·2	14·7	15·8	16·3	17·4	17·9	

Square M–M1.

M–M1	1·0	1·3	1·9	2·0	1·5	1·7	1·8	2·3	1·7	1·6	
I–N	7·0	7·0	7·5	7·5	7·0	8·0	8·0	8·5	10	10·5	

Sizes 92–110
Connect I–N–M1 to complete the waist.

N–O					9·5	10	10·5	11	11·5	12	*depth of dart*
N–N1					0·5	0·5	0·7	0·7	1·0	1·0	*width of front dart*
N–N2					0·5	0·5	0·8	0·8	1·0	1·0	

Sizes 116–146
  Square N–O.
Connect I–N1–O–N2–M1 to complete the waist.
Connect L–H to complete the sideseam and hem in
a similar manner to the back skirt.

For sizes 92–110, the British Standards measurements are identical for boys and girls and the basic blocks can be used for both sexes. From size 116 they apply to girls only, but providing some small adjustments are made, they can be adapted for boy's basic blocks. This is possible because the differences are so slight, as shown by the figures in the chart these can be compared with those in the British Standards Chart on page 12.

	BOYS AND GIRLS				BOYS					
SIZE	92	98	104	110	116	122	128	134	140	146
CHEST	56	57	58·5	60	61	63·5	66	68·5	72	74
WAIST	52	53	54	55	57	58	61	64	66	68
HIPS	56·5	59	61	63·5	66	68	71·5	75	78	80

The chest measurements remain the same while in some of the larger sizes the waist increases and the hips decrease in size. These differences are reflected in the alterations made to the basic bodice and trouser blocks. The sleeve block for both boys and girls remains the same.

BOY'S BASIC BODICE BLOCK

Construct the block in exactly the same manner as that for the girl's block except for the following alterations.

SIZE	92	98	104	110	116	122	128	134	140	146
K–M	19·2	19·9	20·6	21·8	23	23·7	24·9	25·6	26·8	28
Q–QI	0·5	0·5	0·6	0·6	0·7	0·7	0·8	0·8	0·9	0·9

Q–Q2 equals Q–QI.

Do not construct the back or front darts. To complete the waist shaping connect M–QI and B–Q2 using points X and V as guide points. See diagram 3 on page 14.

Although for sizes 92–110 the girl's basic trouser block can be used because the cut of the larger sizes is different, it is worthwhile reconstructing the smaller sizes as well. Older boys have slightly larger waists and narrower hips than girls of a similar size, but even where the measurements are identical, the shape is distributed differently. A boy's stomach is flatter and therefore no darting is needed in the front block to provide fullness over a stomach curve. Most of the shaping is confined to the back block and a more pronounced crotch seam helps to reduce some of the extra fullness needed for the buttock area. The rest is taken out by a back dart which is shorter than that in the girl's trouser block because of the higher shaped buttocks. The sideseam is moved forward 1 cm so that it will not appear off-centre, a possibility caused by the redistribution of the shaping.

Draft   Diagram 12
Construct a rectangle to the following dimensions leaving a 10 cm extension all round.

SIZE	92	98	104	110	116	122	128	134	140	146	
WIDTH	34·2	35·5	36·5	37·7	39	40	41·7	43·5	45	46	
LENGTH	54	58	62	66	70	74	78	82	86	90	

Halve the rectangle vertically with a temporary line.

Make the line A–B 1 cm to the right of this line and mark the following points on it.

A–C	10·5	11	12	12·5	13·5	14	15	15·5	16·5	17	*depth of waist to hip*
A–D	18	19	20	21	22	23	24·5	25·5	27	28	*body rise plus ease*
includes	+1	+1	+1	+1	+1	+1	+1·5	+1·5	+1·5	+1·5	*ease*

E midway between C–B.

Square points C,D,E to the edges of the rectangle extending D at least 10 cm beyond the rectangle each side.

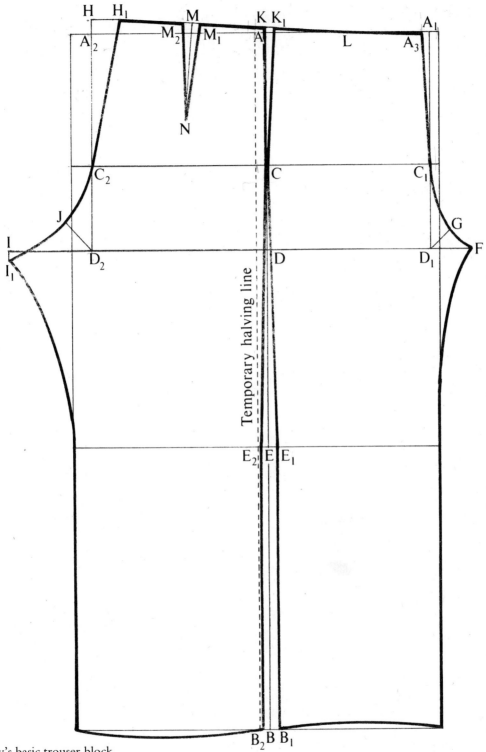

Temporary halving line

12   Boy's basic trouser block

Crotch shaping front

SIZE	92	98	104	110	116	122	128	134	140	146	
A–A1	15·1	15·8	16·3	16·9	17·5	18	18·9	19·8	20·5	21	

C–C1 equals A–A1. D–D1 equals A–A1.
Connect A1–C1–D1.

	92	98	104	110	116	122	128	134	140	146	
D1–F	3·6	3·8	4·0	4·2	4·4	4·6	4·8	5·0	5·2	5·4	
D1–G	2·0	2·2	2·4	2·6	2·8	3·0	3·2	3·4	3·6	3·8	*D1–G bisects the angle*

Connect F–G–C1 to A3, which is 0·5 cm to the
left of A1, to complete the front crotch shape.

Crotch shaping back

A –A2	16·1	16·7	17·2	17·8	18·5	19	19·8	20·7	21·5	22	

C–C2 equals A–A2. D–D2 equals C–C2.
Connect D2–C2–A2 extending the line A2 to
H.
Square H to H1.

	92	98	104	110	116	122	128	134	140	146	
A2–H	1·0	1·1	1·2	1·3	1·4	1·5	1·6	1·7	1·8	1·9	
H–H1	1·3	1·5	2·1	2·7	2·9	3·1	3·3	3·3	3·3	3·3	
D2–I	8·1	8·3	8·5	8·7	8·9	9·1	9·3	9·5	9·7	9·9	
D2–J	3·3	3·5	3·7	3·8	3·9	4·1	4·3	4·5	4·7	4·9	*D2–J bisects the angle*

I1 is 0·5 cm below I.
Connect points I1–J–C2–H1 to complete the
back crotch shape.

Waist shaping front
Extend line A–B to K and square K–K1.

	92	98	104	110	116	122	128	134	140	146	
A–K	0·3	0·4	0·4	0·4	0·5	0·5	0·5	0·5	0·6	0·6	
K–K1	0·5	0·5	0·5	0·5	0·7	0·7	0·7	0·7	0·7	0·7	

L is midway between A–A1.
Connect C–K1–L–A3 to form the front shaping.

Waist shaping back
Connect H1–K and midway on this line mark point M.

Square M–N and mark off the dart width.

SIZE	92	98	104	110	116	122	128	134	140	146	
M–N		8·5	9·0	9·5	10	10·5	11	11·5	12	12·5	*depth of dart*
M–M1		0·7	0·7	0·7	0·7	0·7	0·7	1·0	1·2	1·2	*width of dart*
M–M2		0·8	0·8	0·8	0·8	0·8	0·8	1·0	1·3	1·3	

Connect H1–M2–N–M1–K to form the back shaping.

Leg shaping
E–E1, E–E2, B–B1, B–B2 are all equal.

E–E1	0·5	0·6	0·7	0·8	0·9	1·0	1·1	1·2	1·3	1·4	

Connect K1–C–E1–B1 to establish the front side seam.

Connect K–C–E2–B2 to establish the back side seam.

Join F and I1 to the main construction lines above the kneeline as shown in diagram 12 to complete the inside seam shape. Curve the back hemline 0·5 cm below the baseline and the front hemline 0·5 cm above the baseline for a shaped hem.

Section 3 Construction of secondary blocks from the bodice block

Fitted basic blocks are the framework around which other useful blocks can be constructed. The major advantage in constructing these subsidiary blocks is the amount of time saved if one particular garment is going to be used many times. If a pattern cutter intends to work around a panelled type of garment then it is easier to have a panelled block available than to draft a new one every time a different style is started. A designer of coats and jackets would similarly use a coat block although fitted blocks should be available if ever any measurements need to be compared with the originals.

The secondary blocks in this section are those used as a foundation for many of the styles frequently seen in children's clothes. These are the simple dress block, a panelled block and a coat block. They are all adaptions of the basic bodice block in the previous section. The length of each block is that of the cervical to the knee. This gives a rather long and old-fashioned appearance but because it is a British Standards measurement it is an excellent basic guideline. Any hem length required can be adjusted from this standard.

FULL LENGTH SIMPLE DRESS BLOCK
DIAGRAM 13

The waist area of most children, particularly smaller ones, is not normally their best feature, and the cut of this block is designed to disguise it. The shaping is not in the true waist area but mid-way between the waist and chest lines, giving a higher waisted effect. This enables the block to skim over the least flattering area of children and also results in a basic style which is more suitably shaped for an active child. The sideseams are curved in under the arms, following the lines of the basic block and giving a neater fit with less bulk at this point than a line taken straight from the under arm to the hemline.

Draft
Construct a rectangle to the appropriate measurements. Align the front and back basic blocks in the positions shown after first establishing the chest line from the back bodice block. Trace round both blocks and remove.

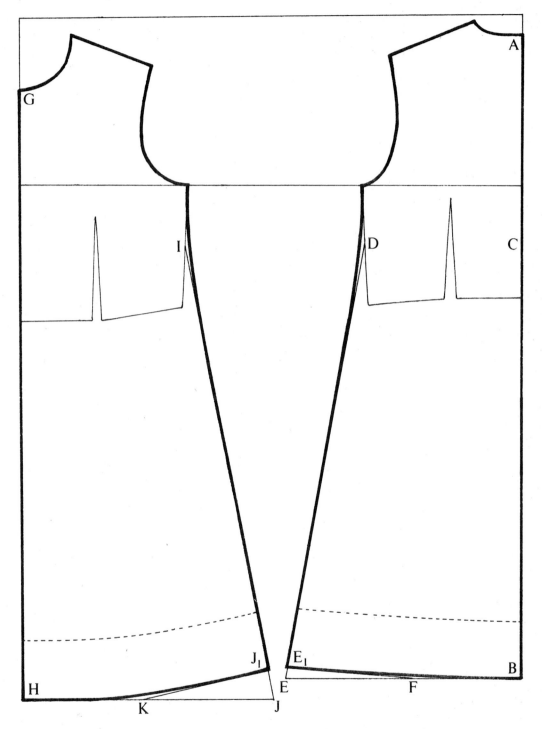

13   Simple dress block

SIZE	92	98	104	110	116	122	128	134	140	146
LENGTH	61	64	67	71	75	79	82	86	90	94
WIDTH	47	48	50	51	53	55	57	59	62	64
A–B	·51	54	57	61	65	69	72	76	80	84
B–E	22·5	23·2	24	24·7	25·3	26·1	27·1	28·3	29·4	30·7
G–H	48·7	51·4	54·1	57·8	61·5	65·2	67·9	71·6	75·3	79
H–J	23·2	24	24·7	25·5	26·4	27·1	28·3	29·4	30·6	32·2

Back

C is midway between the chestline and the waist.

D is a midway point on the bodice sideseam.
Square B to E, see chart, and connect D–E.
D–E1 equals C–B. F is midway on line E–B.
Connect E1–F–B to form the hemline.

Front

I is a midway point on the bodice sideseam.
Square H to J, see chart, and connect I–J.
I–J1 equals C–B. K is midway on line H–J.
Connect J1–H curving the hemline above K.
Curve the sideseams at points D and I to avoid a sharp angle.

Sleeveless variation   Diagram 14

Many summer styles are sleeveless and the block has to be changed in the shoulder-armhole area to allow for this. As the alterations are so slight, they can be drafted straight on to the pattern, if required, instead of making a special block. The armhole is raised and tightened so that there is no unsightly gaping and the shoulder-width is reduced so that the garment edge does not protrude beyond the edge of the body shoulder. Place the back and front blocks in position on the pattern paper ready for drafting and make the following adjustments exactly on both halves.

Point A. At the underarm establish A by measuring 0·5 cm in and 0·5 cm up from the underarm point of the basic block. This measurement is the same for all sizes.

Point B. From the shoulder point reduce the shoulder seam to B by 1 cm for size 92. Increase this measurement by 0·1 cm for each subsequent size. Connect A–B with a new armhole line and join A to the waist area to form a new sideseam.

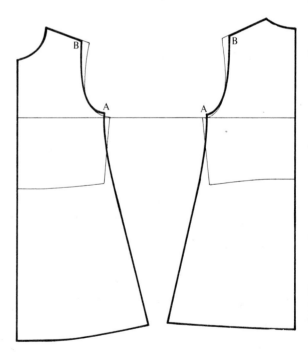

14   Simple sleeveless dress block

36

The styling of this block is based upon the simple dress block and has the shape flaring gently out from under the chest line rather than the waist for sizes 92–104. The seamline formed by the shaped panels make it a flattering style on a chubby child. They are also the basis of the classic panelled coat when constructed on a coat block.

Draft of the panelled block
Construct a rectangle to the appropriate measurements. Align the front and back basic bodice blocks in the position illustrated in diagram 15 after first squaring out the chest line from the back bodice block across the full width of the draft. Trace round both blocks and remove.

Sizes 92–98–104   Diagram 15
The back and front drafts are constructed in exactly the same manner except that some measurements are different.

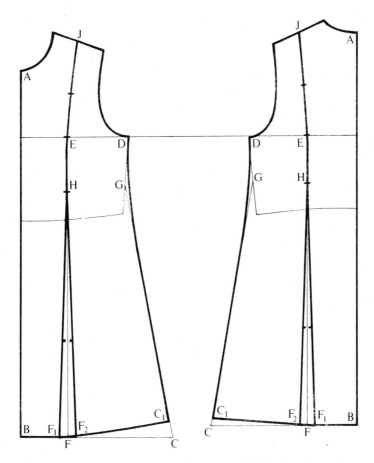

15   Panelled block, sizes 92–104

	BACK				FRONT		
SIZE	92	98	104	SIZE	92	98	104
LENGTH	61	64	67				
WIDTH	47	48	50				
A–B	51	54	57	A–B	48·7	51·4	54·1
	Square B–C				Square B–C		
B–C	20·6	21·2	21·6	B–C	21·5	21·8	22·4
D–E	8·0	8·5	8·5	D–E	8·5	9·0	9·0
	Square E–F				Square E–F		
F–F1	0·5	0·5	0·5	F–F1	0·5	0·5	0·5
F–F2	0·5	0·5	0·5	F–F2	0·5	0·5	0·5
D–G	6·0	6·5	7·0	D–G	6·0	6·5	7·0
E–H	5·9	6·4	6·9	E–H	8·1	8·4	8·7
	Connect G–C				Connect G–C		
G–C1	31·6	33·6	36	G–C1	31·6	33·6	36

Establish point J midway on the shoulder line.
Connect J–E–H–F2 for the centre panel seam.
Connect E–H–F1 for the side panel seam.

Connect D–C1 to establish the sideseam curving the line gently at G.

Connect B–F2 for the hemline of the centre panel.

Connect F1–C1 for the hemline of the side panel.

The bottom of the panels overlap at the hemline so it is necessary to transfer the pattern onto card using a tracing wheel. Before doing so, mark balance notches at points E, H, midway between E–J, and midway between H–F1 and H–F2.

Sizes 110–146   Diagram 16
Align and trace onto drafting card as for the previous sizes.

Back

SIZE	110	116	122	128	134	140	146
LENGTH	71	75	79	82	86	90	94
WIDTH	51	53	55	57	59	61	64
A–B	61	65	69	72	76	80	84

Square B–C.

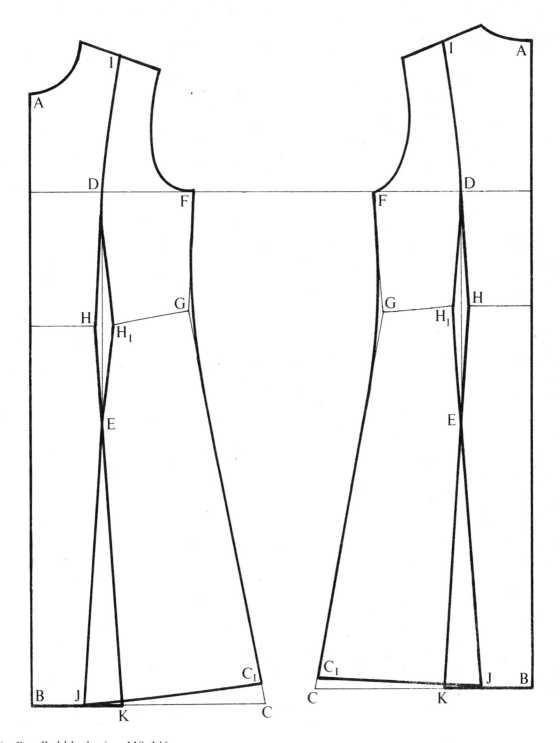

16   Panelled block, sizes 110–146

SIZE	110	116	122	128	134	140	146
B–C	23	23·6	24·1	25·2	26·1	27·3	28·1
D–E	22·1	23·4	24·5	25·8	27	28·7	30

Square D–E through the centre of the dart.

F is the underarm point.

G is the sidewaist point. Connect G–C.

C–C1 measures 0·5 cm for size 110 and increases 0·1 cm for each subsequent size.

H is the inside dart point. H1 is the outside dart point.

Establish point I midway on the shoulder line.

Connect I–D and continue the line through the top of the dart to H.

Connect H–K, on the line B–C, with a straight line passing through E to establish the centre panel seam edge.

From the top of the dart join H1–J, on the line B–C, with a straight line passing through E to establish the side panel seam.

Curve the lines at H and H1 to soften the dart angle if necessary.

Join F–C1 to form the sideseam, curving the line at G to eliminate the angular waistline.

Join C1–J for the hemline of the side panel.

Transfer the panels to a piece of card and insert balance points at appropriate places.

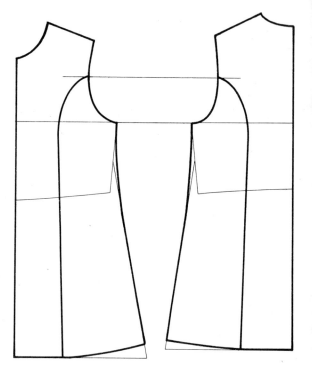

17   Panelled block, wing seam variation

Front

SIZE	110	116	122	128	134	140	146
A–B	57·8	61·5	65·2	67·9	71·6	75·3	79
Square B–C							
B–C	23·9	25	25·5	26·7	27·5	28·3	30
D–E	21·9	23·1	24·1	25·2	26·3	28	29·1

Square D–E through the centre of the dart.

F is the underarm point. G is the sidewaist point. Connect G–C.

G–C1 equals G–C1 on the back block. From this point repeat the instructions given for the back draft.

Diagram 17

This shows how the seam can be varied by curving it into the armhole to form a wing seam. This is sometimes known as a 'Princess line' pattern.

STRAIGHT COAT BLOCK

The important point of any coat block is not so much the styling lines which are variable, but the extra tolerances allowed for above those already drafted into the basic block. These are essential because a coat is usually worn over some other form of clothing. If no allowances are made, the fit would always be extremely tight and uncomfortable. In this construction, extra width is made through the shoulder area, armhole and around the chest, proportionate to the size being drafted.

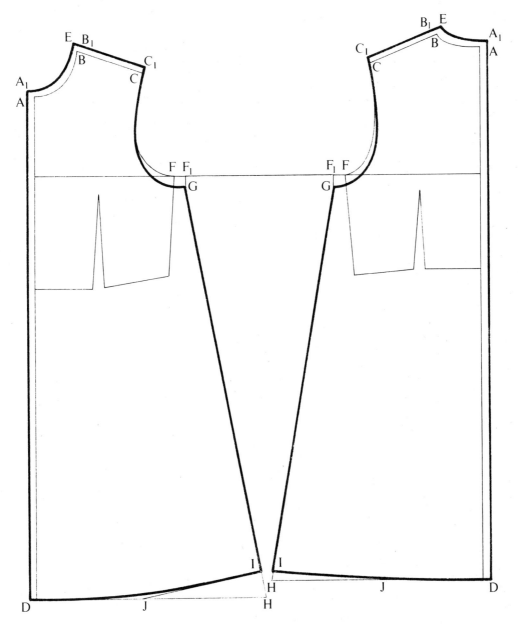

18   Coat block

Coat block draft   Diagram 18

The back and front basic blocks are aligned along the chest line as in the previous constructions, but make the centre back and centre front lines at least 2 cm inside the edges of the rectangle. Mark points A, B, C, D in the positions shown, and establish A–D by adding extra ease to the centre back. For amount of ease, see chart.

SIZE	92	98	104	110	116	122	128	134	140	146
LENGTH	61	64	67	71	75	79	82	86	90	94
WIDTH	51	52	54	55	57	59	61	63	64	68
EASE	1·0	1·0	1·0	1·0	1·1	1·1	1·1	1·1	1·2	1·2
A–D	51	54	57	61	65	69	72	76	80	84

Extend A–A1 to form new back neck line.
Square B to B1 and C to C1.

A–A1	0·3	0·3	0·3	0·3	0·4	0·4	0·4	0·4	0·5	0·5
B–B1 C–C1	0·6	0·6	0·6	0·6	0·8	0·8	0·8	0·8	1·0	1·0

Connect B1–C1 to form a new shoulder line and extend it beyond B1 to E.

B1–E	0·6	0·6	0·6	0·6	0·7	0·7	0·7	0·7	0·8	0·8

Join E–A1 to make a new back neckline using the old neckline shape as a guide. On the chestline, mark off F–F1. Square F1–G.

F–F1	1·0	1·0	1·1	1·1	1·3	1·3	1·3	1·4	1·4	1·5
F1–G	1·2	1·2	1·3	1·3	1·4	1·4	1·4	1·5	1·5	1·6

Connect G–C1 to form the enlarged armhole, using the old armhole shape as a guide.
Square D–H and connect G–H.
Mark off H–I and join I–J to form the hemline. J is midway on line D–H.

D–H	24·7	25·4	26·2	26·9	27·8	28·6	29·6	30·8	32·2	33·5
H–I	0·5	0·6	0·7	0·8	0·9	1·0	1·1	1·2	1·3	1·4

Front

Mark points A, B, C and D in the positions shown and establish A–D by adding extra ease to the centre front. For ease see chart.

SIZE	92	98	104	110	116	122	128	134	140	146
EASE	1·0	1·0	1·0	1·0	1·1	1·1	1·1	1·1	1·2	1·2
A–D	48·7	51·4	54·1	57·8	61·5	65·2	67·9	71·6	75·3	79

Extend A–A1 to form a new centre front neck point.

Square B–B1 and C–C1.

A–A1	0·3	0·3	0·3	0·3	0·4	0·4	0·4	0·4	0·5	0·5
B–B1 C–C1	0·6	0·6	0·6	0·6	0·8	0·8	0·8	0·8	1·0	1·0

Join B1–C1 to form a new shoulder line and extend it beyond B1 to E.

B1–E	0·6	0·6	0·6	0·6	0·7	0·7	0·7	0·7	0·8	0·8

Connect E–A1 to form the new front neckline using the old line as a guide line. On the chest line mark off F–F1. Square F1–G.

F–F1	1·0	1·0	1·1	1·1	1·3	1·3	1·3	1·4	1·4	1·5
F1–G	1·2	1·2	1·3	1·3	1·4	1·4	1·4	1·5	1·5	1·6

Join G–C1 to form the new armhole shape. Square D–H and join G–H.

D–H	25·4	26·2	26·9	27·7	28·9	29·6	30·8	31·9	33·4	35

Make G–I equal G–I on the back block.

J is midway on line D–H.

Connect I–J to form the hemline curving it as shown in diagram 18. By extending and lowering the basic block at the underarm, and raising the shoulder, the size of the armhole has increased in width and length. This can vary from 4·5 cm in the smaller sizes to about 6·5 cm in the larger ones. A corresponding increase must be made to the basic sleeve block, otherwise it will be too small to fit the new armhole correctly. Instructions for this alteration are given in the following section, on sleeve types.

Section 4   *Construction of Secondary sleeve blocks and variations*

Other than the instructions for a new basic sleeve to fit the coat block and a two-piece sleeve block which is based on it, all the sleeve variations in this section are drafted from the basic bodice sleeve. For any style which is going to be used frequently, it can be useful to make a set of subsidary blocks such as the semi-fitted, raglan or two-piece sleeve. Ensure that the correct basic sleeve is being altered to fit the correct basic block. It would be frustrating to realise that the raglan sleeve pattern just drafted for a coat, did not fit because it had been incorrectly taken from the bodice sleeve block.

STRAIGHT COAT SLEEVE BLOCK

DIAGRAM 19

Unless it is altered as a styling feature, one point which distinguishes the coat sleeve from many others is its lack of tightness at the wrist, and its easy fit throughout its length. This enables it to be worn comfortably over other sleeves. It is constructed by making simple alterations to the basic sleeve block. Extra width is allowed through-out its length and the underarm points are dropped to give an easier fit around the armhole area.

Draft

Construct a rectangle for the correct size and halve vertically. Centre the basic sleeve block on this line, and mark points A and B at the sleevehead and hem of the block. Point A should be about 0·5 cm from the top of the rectangle.

Square out a line through the underarm points and use these lines as a guide.

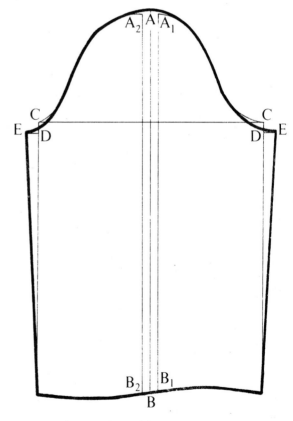

19   Straight coat sleeve block

44

SIZE	92	98	104	110	116	122	128	134	140	146
WIDTH	24	25	26	27	28	29	30	31	32	33
LENGTH	33	35	37	39	41	43	45	48	50	53
A–A1 A–A2	0·6	0·6	0·6	0·6	0·8	0·8	0·8	0·8	1·0	1·0
C–D	1·0	1·0	1·1	1·1	1·3	1·3	1·3	1·4	1·4	1·5
D–E	1·2	1·2	1·3	1·3	1·4	1·4	1·4	1·5	1·5	1·6

Establish point A1 by moving the block outwards to the right keeping it parallel to the centre line A–B. Trace round the right-hand half.

Repeat on the left hand side of the block to A2.

At the underarm mark points C.

Measure C–D and square D–E.

Connect E–A1 and E–A2 through the balance points to establish the new sleevehead shape. If the sleevehead appears too flat, raise A slightly and join the new crown point smoothly into the sleevehead.

Connect E to the hem and re-draw the hemline to remove any flatness at B.

TWO-PIECE SLEEVE DIAGRAMS 20A, B AND C

This sleeve is normally found in outerwear, coats, jackets and blazers and is useful as a subsidary sleeve block constructed to fit the coat block. It consists of a top-sleeve and a slightly smaller under-sleeve. This enables the curved seamlines, which give the sleeve its shape, to hang towards the inside of the sleeve.

Draft Diagram 20a

Align the basic coat sleeve block on the line A–B and trace round. Straighten the under-arm seams so that they are parallel with each other.

Measure A–C to establish the elbow level.

From C square to C1 and C2 on the sleeve edges to form the elbow line.

D is midway on line C–C1 and E is midway on line C–C2. Measure D–F.

Square F to A1 and B1. Square E to A2 and B2.

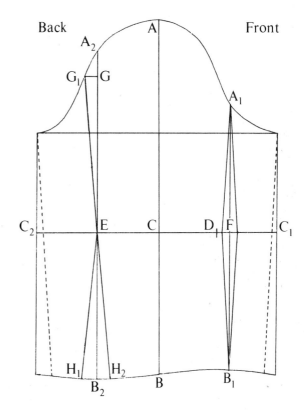

20a Two-piece sleeve, basic construction

45

SIZE	92	98	104	110	116	122	128	134	140	146
A–C	18·8	19·6	20·6	21·7	22·9	24·2	25·4	26·8	28·1	29·6
D–F	1·0	1·1	1·2	1·3	1·4	1·5	1·6	1·7	1·8	1·9
G–G1	0·7	0·8	0·9	1·0	1·1	1·2	1·3	1·4	1·5	1·6
B2–H1 B2–H2	1·5	1·5	1·6	1·6	1·7	1·7	1·8	1·8	1·9	1·9

On line C–C1 measure 1 cm either side of F. Connect these points to A1 and B1. Using these lines as a guideline establish the seam lines with a slight curve.

On line E–A2 at the sleevehead square G–G1 until it meets the sleeve head at the correct length.

Establish points H on the hemline measuring from B2.

Connect G1–E, E–H2. Curve the line G1–E–H1 at E to eliminate the angle.

Diagram 20b
Cut G1–E–H1 and trim away the shaded areas shown in the diagram. Join the underarm seams together to form the under-sleeve as indicated by the dotted line.

Diagram 20c
Place both parts of the pattern onto a sheet of card and accurately trace off the final pattern. Put in balance marks as illustrated.

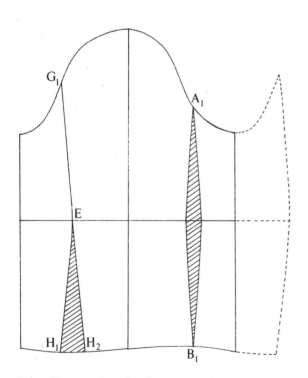

20b Construction showing areas to be cut away

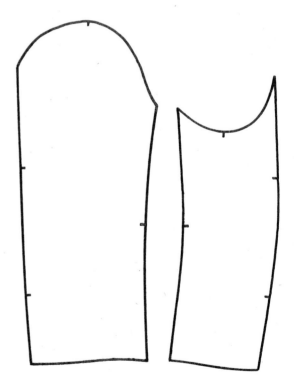

20c Completed block with balance marks

This sleeve is used quite often for coats, jackets and dresses to give a more fitted shape than the basic block. Some designers and pattern cutters sometimes prefer to use it as the basic sleeve block. See Diagrams 21a and b.

SIZE	92	98	104	110	116	122	128	134	140	146
A–C	18·8	19·6	20·6	21·7	22·9	24·5	25·4	26·8	28·1	29·6
D–D1	1·0	1·1	1·1	1·2	1·2	1·3	1·3	1·4	1·4	1·5

Centre the basic sleeve block onto pattern paper and trace round.

Mark in points A and B to establish the centre line of the sleeve.

Measure A–C. Square C to D. Mark points E, 1 cm inside the sleeve edges for all sizes.

Connect points E to the underarm points. Measure D–F, two-thirds of the length of C–D.

Square F to G on hemline.

Cut lines D–F and G–F so that this section can pivot at F.

Before pivoting, trim off the shaded areas.

Open dart D–D1 by moving G towards B. Re-draw the hemline into a smooth shape. Measure the underarm to dart length and transfer it to the other side to establish a balance point.

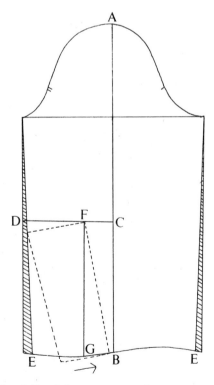

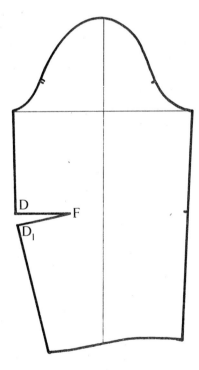

21a   Semi-fitted sleeve construction   21b

This sleeve is used a lot in children's wear because of its easy-fitting qualities. Although it tends to emphasize a sloping shoulder, something an adult would not generally wish to do, this very fact makes it a good style on the many children whose shoulders have not yet developed. Two types are given here: the high and the low raglan.

The fit of a high raglan is similar to that of a set-in sleeve. The shape of the lower part of the bodice armhole, and the corresponding part of the sleevehead remains unaltered, keeping their usual fit. The cut and shape of the raglan is developed above these points. This makes this particular raglan variation suited to a more fitted sleeve generally found in dresses and blouses.

The low raglan is less fitted around the underarm area and allows extra amounts of ease and width to be built into a garment. For this reason it is frequently found in children's coats where movement and tolerance is very necessary. Of course, this does not exclude its use for easy-fitting dresses or smocks.

The raglan sleeve is constructed by using the sleeve and bodice blocks together and the basic principle of both types is very simple. The top part of the raglan, which on the bodice is above a style line extending from the armhole to the neck, must be separated and attached to the crown of the sleeve.

High raglan sleeve   Diagrams 22a and b
Establishing a pleasing and aesthetic line from the armhole to the neckline is the most difficult part when constructing a raglan sleeve and there is no substitute for practice and experience. The point at which the style line leaves the armhole will determine the whole look of the sleeve. This construction is just one of the many style variations which are possible.

Diagram 22a
Equalize the shoulder lengths by cutting off the 0·5 cm ease on the back shoulder seam at the armhole. On the back bodice block make the neck point to A measurement, approximately

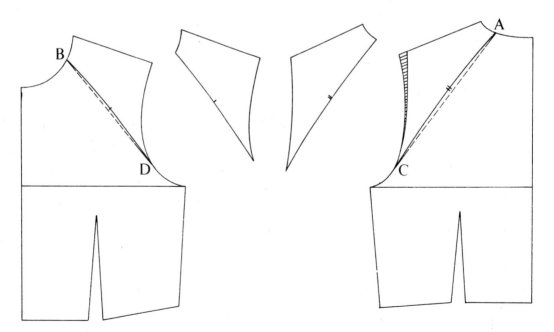

22a   High fitting raglan sleeve, panel separation

one-third of the half-back neck length. On the front bodice block make the neck point to B equal to the similar back measurement.

Connect A and B to the armhole with a straight line which runs naturally into the curved part of the armhole. This is the broken line in the diagram.

Midway on these lines measure out on the shoulder seam side 0·5 cm.

Using this point as a guide connect A and B to their respective armholes with a good curved line. Where this line meets the armhole, which might be slightly above the original lines from A and B, mark C and D as shown.

Put in balance marks and separate the raglan panels from the bodice by cutting along lines A–C and B–D.

Diagram 22b

On a sheet of paper a third longer than the sleeve length, trace round the sleeve block.

Mark points C and D equal in measurement from the underarm to their corresponding points on the front and back bodice blocks.

Take the front and back panels and position them on the sleeve C to C and D to D. At points C and D, pivot the panels so that their shoulder points touch the top of the sleeve crown.

Extend the shoulder lines to complete the V-shape. This is the shoulder seam part of a one piece raglan sleeve and can be slashed and altered to give the sleeve more variations if needed. To avoid poking at the end of the seam, the seam can be curved to an appropriate point below the bottom of the V. This is indicated by the broken line.

Sellotape the parts firmly together and transfer the sleeve to another sheet of card or paper to be traced round and cut out.

Make points C and D on both the sleeve and bodice blocks into balance marks as a further guide.

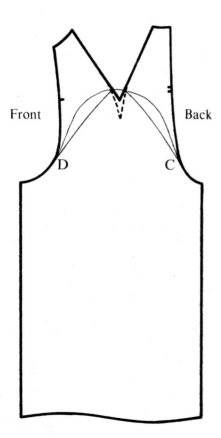

Front   Back

22b   Completed sleeve block

Low raglan sleeve. Diagrams 23a, b and c
The interpretation of the style line from the neck to the underarm is of prime importance. The method given here is only one of the many variations which can be made. The instructions are for both the front and back bodice.

Diagram 23a
Trace round the basic bodice blocks or the appropriate part of the coat block being used. At the armhole, remove the ease, 0·5 cm, from the back shoulder to equalize the shoulder seam lengths.

At the neckline make the neck point to A measurement approximately one-third of the neck length to establish point A.

To deepen the armhole, measure down from the underarm point at least 2·5 cm, for size 92 increasing this by 0·2 cm per size. Size 146 should therefore be 4·5 cm. Draw a line parallel to the lower section of the armhole equal in distance from it to the deepened underarm measurement.

At an appropriate cut-off point, establish point B and connect to A. This is the broken line in the diagram.

Midway along line A–B measure out 1·0 cm on the shoulder seam side and use this point as a guide to join A–B with a curved line. If a very curved style line is needed, it will probably be better to move point B nearer the armhole, though this will naturally depend upon the exact nature of the curve that is being established. Place in balance marks at appropriate points along the style lines.

Diagram 23b
On a sheet of paper one-third longer than the sleeve length, trace round the sleeve block, and extend the top arm line through the underarm points.

From the armhole edge of the panels slash towards the style line edge. Do this about every centimetre, but do not cut through the style line edge or past the armhole balance mark.

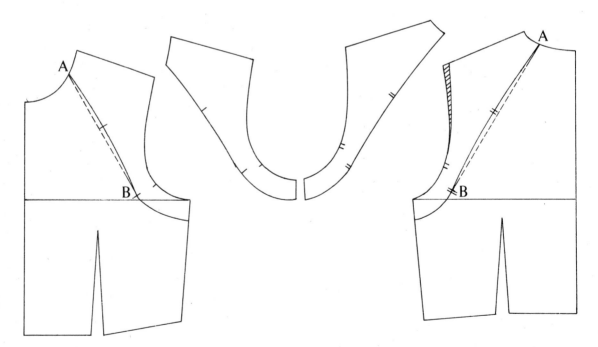

23a   Low fitting raglan sleeve

Put the armhole and sleeve balance points together and from these points pivot the sections so that their shoulder points touch the top of the sleeve crown. Complete the V-shaped shoulder seam.

Diagram 23c
Draw a parallel line above the underarm points the same distance as the underarm was lowered at the side seam.

Using this line as a guide spread the raglan panels open, thus widening and lengthening the sleeve to allow for the shortening of the bodice block at the underarm.

The front curve will be more shaped than the back because the basic sleeve and bodice block shapes are more cut away in this area. Do not try to make them exactly alike, but let them fall naturally into position on the guide line.

Connect the new underarm points to the sleeve hem. If the sleeve appears to be too wide, join the underarm points to the sleeve seam at the elbow level. In both cases if an inward curving seam is introduced it will narrow the sleeve a little more.

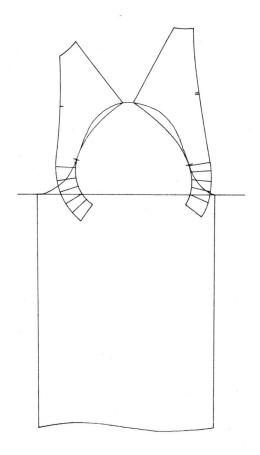

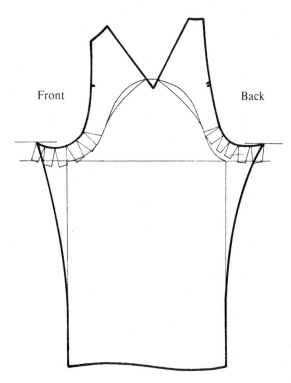

Front   Back

23b   Placement of panels prior to cutting

23c   Spreading of panels to complete the sleeve block

51

Diagram 24
For the two-piece sleeve, separate the sleeve into two parts by cutting from the point of the shoulder dart to the hem. Curve the seam line in the shoulder area to eliminate any angles caused by cutting. Put balance marks on the new seam line. If extra sleeve width is necessary, add an equal amount to the outside seamlines curving them in at the shoulder point where the shoulder seam begins.

Diagram 25
Fullness can be added by slashing from the hem to the end of the shoulder seam dart and pivoting this point to bring the neck points together. The fullness will have been inserted at the sleeve hem. If less fullness is required do not completely close the shoulder dart.

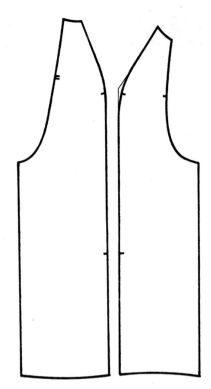

24   Two-part raglan

25   Wide-sleeved raglan with closed dart

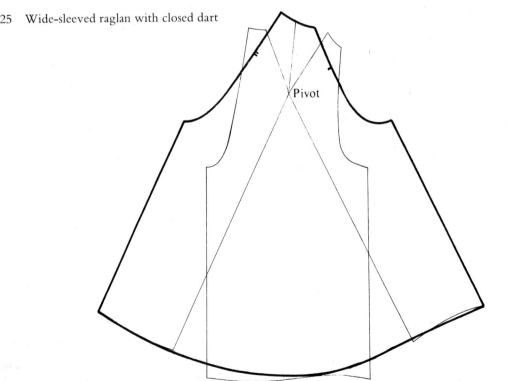

Pivot

ADDITION OF EXTRA FULLNESS

At this point it is appropriate to introduce 'slashing'. This is the process by which a pattern piece can be cut (slashed) and altered so that extra fullness and shaping can be introduced where needed.

A pattern can be cut and separated completely so that fullness is added throughout its whole length. Cuts can also be made from one edge to within a couple of millimetres of another edge. In this case the cut edge is spread open while the length of the uncut edge remains the same although its shape will alter. The following sleeve styles illustrate both methods. If the extra fullness is needed throughout the whole of the pattern spread the cuts evenly, but if it is required in one part only make the cuts in the appropriate places.

STYLE VARIATIONS FROM THE BASIC SLEEVE BLOCK

Full puff sleeve   Diagrams 26a, b and c
The sleeve is slashed throughout its width so that it can be gathered into the armhole and a simple cuff band.

Bell sleeve   Diagrams 27a, b and c   Bishop sleeve Diagrams 27a, b and d
Both these sleeves have width added in the same manner and the length of the sleevehead remains unaltered. The broken line, diagram 27b, indicates the extra length added for the blousing effect of the bishop sleeve. It can be made fuller if needed.

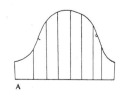

26 Puff sleeve. *a* position of slashes,
b spreading of pattern, *c* made up sleeve

27 Bell and bishop sleeves. *a* positioning of slashes for both sleeves, *b* spreading of pattern, *c* bell sleeve, *d* bishop sleeve

Leg-o-mutton sleeve   Diagrams 28a, b and c
This sleeve shows the manner in which extra
fullness is put into the sleevehead only. This can
be eased or darted into the armhole. It is usual for
this sleeve to fit at the wrist so the fitted sleeve
block would make a more appropriate foundation
for this style.

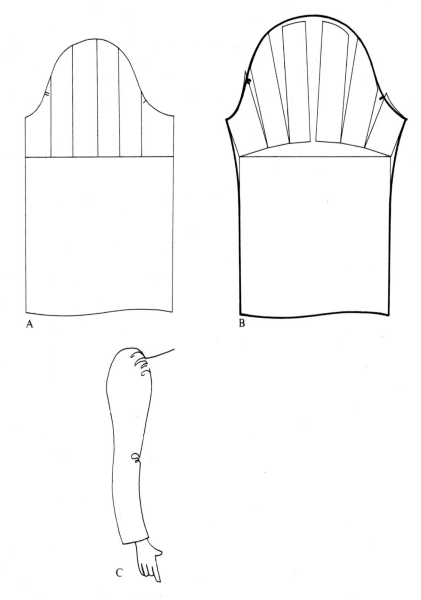

28   Leg-o'-mutton sleeve. *a* position of slashes,
     b spreading of pattern, *c* made up sleeve

Cuffs

Sleeves can be made more interesting by the addition of cuffs, which can be straight, in which case the depth should be less than the halfway distance between the wrist and the elbow, or shaped. A shaped cuff is usually a deep cuff and is wider at the top edge, either because of the greater width of the arm or to achieve a flared-out effect.

If a plain cuff without a fastening is required, its circumference must be sufficient to pull over the widest part of the hand. An open style can be made to fit much more tightly. Its length should be the circumference of the arm where it is required to fit, plus 2 or 3 cm ease, plus the width of a buttonwrap, if needed.

The length of a sleeve can be reduced by the width of cuff or, if it is required to blouse out over a cuff, the length would be reduced less so that the ease is included for the amount of blousing needed.

Shaped cuff   Diagrams 29a, b and c
A rectangle of pattern paper is slashed and widened sufficiently so that the widest edge will fit around the wider part of the arm.

Simple cuff styles   Diagrams 30a, b, c and d
The first three styles are for open cuffs. Style 30d is flared out and would look better on a shorter sleeve.

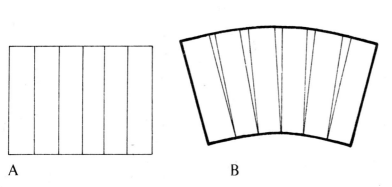

A   B   C

29   Slashing for a cuff. *a* position of slashes,
     b spreading of pattern, *c* typical shaped cuff

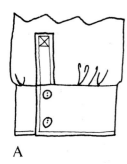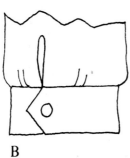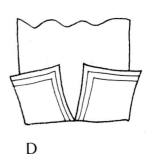

A   B   C   D

30a–d   Simple cuff styles

Section 5   Trousers

Most trouser variations for children evolve around differing leg shapes, leg lengths and waist extensions. They are all simple to construct although some are basically for children in the 92–110 size range. It is usual to have the back waist of any style in this size range elasticated. Apart from holding trousers up and keeping tops tucked in, it does not cause any restriction at the waist and is very comfortable for a small child. The waist of the block is the natural waistline so if a hipster style is needed the excess can be evenly cut from the pattern when the style is being drafted. The styles can be used for boys or girls, although the diagrams are from the boy's block.

DUNGAREES   SIZE APPROXIMATELY 92–110

The draft for dungarees requires a small extension to the front trouser block. This can be made in two ways, either by the addition above the waist of a separate bib section or by extending the front trouser block above the waist.

Separate bib style   Diagram 31
Ignore any darts in the front bodice block and draft on the required shape of the bib using the front bodice block as a guideline. Put the shoulders of the front and back blocks together to determine the length and position of the straps which should cross over at the back. (See diagram 46 in the skirt section.) The back trouser block remains unaltered.

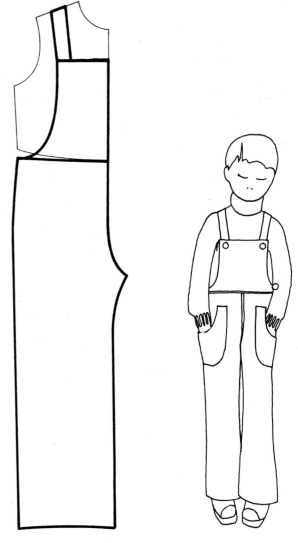

31   Dungarees, separate bib style

Extended bib style   Diagram 32

Trace round the front trouser block and extend the crotch line at the waist. Place the front bodice block to this line so that the shape and size of the bib can be drafted onto the trouser section. Ignore any darts in the bodice or trouser blocks. Establish the straps in the same manner as the separate bib style. The back trouser block remains unaltered.

Align the front and back trouser blocks along a common kneeline with their sideseams touching at the hip. Trace round the blocks as far as the kneeline and remove. Join the bottom crotch points to the kneeline. Midway along these lines establish points A and B. Midway along the front kneeline make point C. Square a line from A to meet a line squared from C, establishing point D. From D, square a line to cross the sideseams and to meet a line squared from B at point E. Curve points D and E, for a better shaped hem, to complete the draft.

Shorts with straps   Size approximately 92–110 Diagram 34

Draft a pattern for short trousers and extend the front crotch line. Place the front bodice block to this line and construct the style shown in the diagram. The straps are drafted in the same manner as those in the separate bib dungaree style. The back waist is elasticated.

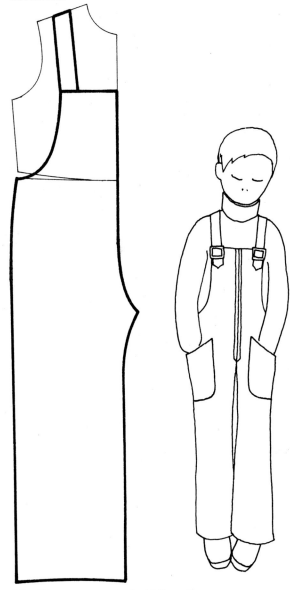

32   Dungarees, extended bib style

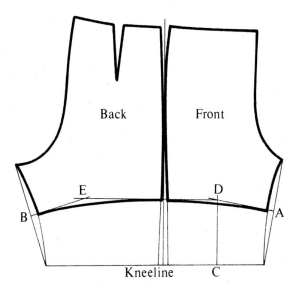

33   Short trouser draft

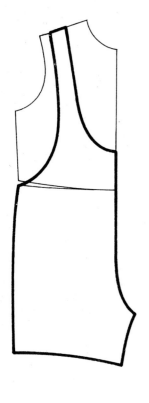

34 Shorts with straps

This is not a tight-fitting cat-suit, but more a one-piece cover-all garment. It is best made in stretch jersey or similar fabrics.

Trace round the front trouser block. Place the centre waist point of the front bodice block to the centre waist point of the trouser block. Pivot the bodice block so that the waistlines of the blocks meet towards the sideseam. The sideseams will not coincide exactly because of the different ease allowances. Connect the underarm point of the bodice block to the hipline of the trouser block with a good curve.

Draft the back of the cat-suit in exactly the same manner. When both have been established, complete the draft by drawing in the style line of the neck and armhole. Make the armhole and neck reasonably large for ease and check that the sideseams and shoulder seams coincide. Elasticate the back waist when making up.

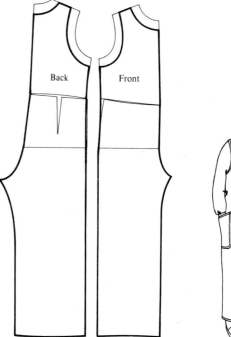

35 Cat-suit

With jeans, the back shaping is put into the yoke by closing up the back dart.

Trace round the back block and from the sideseam construct the yoke style line through the bottom of the dart to the crotch seam. Again from the sideseam, cut up to the dart point and close up the dart. The shaping contained in the back dart has now been transferred into the yoke seamline. If a pocket is required in the front trouser it can coincide with the yoke line at the sideseam.

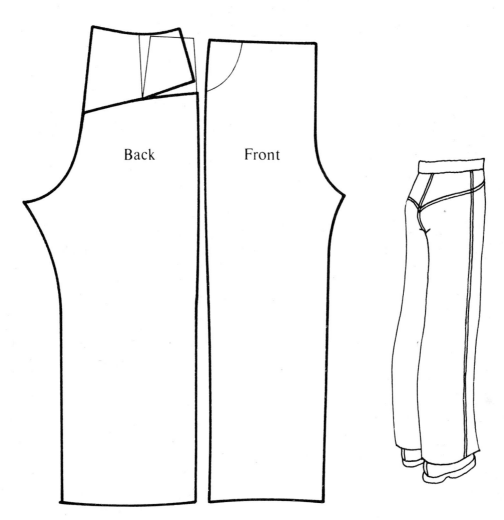

36   Jeans-type trousers

Section 6   Skirts

These should be kept very simple with the minimum of cutting and detail, particularly in the smaller sizes. The skirt block is fairly straight and is not often used in this form except in the larger sizes. Children are very active, and need room in a skirt for movement. This can be achieved by pleats and gathers or by cutting a pattern based on the whole or part of a circle. For smaller sizes, always elasticate the waistband for a better fit.

The measurements in the chart are those most useful for skirt drafting. The first three are British Standards measurements.

CIRCULAR SKIRT   DIAGRAM 37

Whether a circular skirt can be cut completely in one will depend upon the size of the garment, width of the fabric and the making of a satisfactory waist opening. If it is impractical because of material wastage or from a design angle, then side seams can be inserted. The front and back of the skirt are identical, so that only one-half of the skirt needs to be drafted.

Fold a large piece of paper in half so that it is approximately square. The sides should measure the required length of the skirt plus one-sixth of the waist measurement needed. From point A, on the folded edge, square out a line to the edge of the paper. Make A–B one-sixth of the waist measurement and with A–B as a radius pivot at A to establish A–C. The curved line B–C is now approximately one-quarter of the waist size. To draft the hemline mark in the required length, B–D. With A–D as a radius pivot at A to establish A–E. The resulting curved line D–E becomes the

SIZE	92	98	104	110	116	122	128	134	140	146
WAIST	52	53	54	55	57	58	59	61	62	63
HIP	56·5	59	61	63·5	66	68	71·5	75	78·5	83
WAIST TO HIP	10·5	11	12	12·5	13·5	14	15	15·5	16·5	17
WAIST TO KNEE	29	31	33	35	38	40	42	45	48	50
WAIST PLUS EASE	58	59	60	61	61	62	63	65	66	67
FRONT WAIST	27	27·5	28	28·5	29·5	31	31·5	32·5	34	34·5
BACK WAIST	25	25·5	26	26·5	27·5	27	27·5	28·5	28	28·5
HIP PLUS EASE	62·5	65	67	69·5	72	74	77·5	81	84·5	89

hemline. Cut out lines B–C, D–E and B–D. Unfold the paper to form a half pattern. This method allows built-in ease on the waist measurement, but seam and hem allowances must be added. Mark in grain lines and balance points wherever necessary.

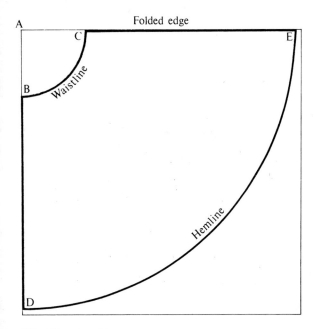

37   Circular skirt

38   Semi-circular skirt

Semi-circular skirt   Diagram 38

This skirt is constructed in a similar manner to the circular style except for a few alterations as shown in the diagram.

Lines A–D, A–E are at right angles to each other, and the sides of the paper, which is not folded, should be the length of the skirt plus one-third of the waist measurement. A–B is one-third of the waist measurement and the curved line B–C is approximately half the waist measurement. The completed draft represents one half of a semi-circular skirt and the angled line indicates the centre back and front lines. This line is constructed by bisecting the angle D–A–E. After cutting out, complete the pattern by adding balance marks, grain lines, seam and hem allowances.

If the back and front waist measurements need to differ, for example, to fit a bodice for a small child, draft separate back and front panels. Use the back and front waist lengths given in the chart and double each one separately before dividing by three to establish the correct A–B length for each half.

Quarter-circle skirt   Diagram 39

This draft is repeated in exactly the same way as that used for the semi-circular style except for the following points: the A–B measurement is two-thirds of the waist measurement. The sides of the pattern paper square are approximately the required skirt length plus the A–B measurement. The completed skirt is the whole pattern, not half. Seams can be inserted wherever necessary.

PLEATED AND GATHERED SKIRTS

Because of their simplicity, not all children's skirts need patterns. The draft can be made directly onto the fabric, which can then be pleated or gathered onto a waistband or bodice. The pleats or gathers are held in position by tacking or gathering threads prior to any permanent stitching. As long as they have been accurately measured and folded into place this should be no problem.

Pleats   Diagram 40a, b and c

A knife pleat is a basic pleat, and is a twice-folded piece of material. The inner fold is hidden by the outer fold and the distance between them is the width of the pleat. The material allowance for a knife pleat is three times its width.

An inverted pleat is two knife pleats folded to meet each other.

A box pleat is an inverted pleat reversed.

For any skirt, it is a simple matter to insert a pleat by slashing through the pattern and spreading it apart to allow for the extra width taken up by the pleat. This is easiest in the centre front and centre back.

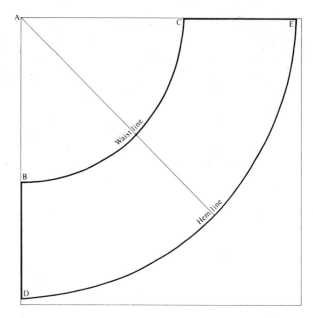

39   Quarter-circle skirt

40   Pleats. *a* knife pleat, *b* inverted pleat,
       c box pleat

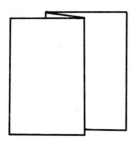
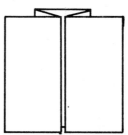
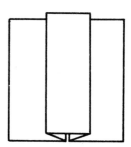

GATHERED SKIRT DIAGRAM 41

This is the simplest skirt of all, but is more suitable for younger children who need less shaping in their clothes. Cut a rectangle of fabric. The width of material is the required length of the skirt and the length approximately twice the hip measurement. This length is variable and depends upon the fabric and effect needed. Finer materials will gather more easily and be less bulky. Add hem and turning allowances. Distribute the fullness evenly, using the gathering foot of the machine, or two gathering threads, and finally insert into the waistband.

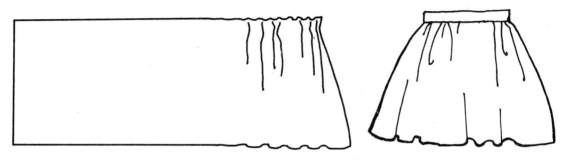

41   Gathered skirt

WAIST PLEATED SKIRT   DIAGRAM 42

A rectangle of fabric is pleated to the required number and width of pleats, held firmly in place by tacking and then attached to the waistband. This works successfully when the outer fold of one pleat is in line with the inner fold of the next pleat as in the diagram. Because they are aligned together in this manner, the length of material needed will always be three times the waist measurement including ease. However it is better to do the calculation below to establish the width and number of pleats which can vary:

Waist divided by the pleat width, multiplied by three times the pleat width.

Example: Size 104, 3 cm pleat
60 divided by 3 equals 20. 20 multiplied by 9 equals 180 which becomes the length of the material required. Add turnings and hem allowances.

42   Waist-pleated skirt

This design is basically similar to the waist pleated skirt except that the pleats are fitted to the hip and then reduced in width to fit the waist. Estimate the number and width of pleats to fit the hip, if possible keeping them even so that the front and back hips have an equal number of pleats. Tack the pleats in position from the hemline to the hip-line. From the hipline the pleats must be reduced in width so that they fit the waistline. They will have to be overlapped more at the back than at the front because the back waist is shorter. To overlap the pleats correctly, divide each reduction amount by the number of pleats being adjusted. Tack each pleat in position before completing the final stitching and attaching to a waistband. The back and front waist measurements are given in the chart in this section. The difference becomes greater as the sizes increase. The example shows how the difference is calculated and the overlap amount if there are ten pleats back and front. Each reduction is small so accuracy is essential.

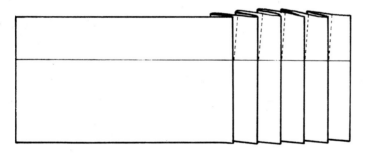

43   Hip-pleated skirt

Example   Size 122

SIZE 122	TOTAL	FRONT	BACK
HIP PLUS EASE	74	37	37
WAIST PLUS EASE	62	33	29
REDUCTION	12	4	8
PLEAT OVERLAP		0·4	0·8
PLEAT WIDTH		3·7	3·7

The kilt is a good style for a child, once they can comfortably wear a skirt, because of its adjustability. It is constructed in a similar manner to a hip pleated skirt except that the ends of the kilt which wrap over and under at the front are left unpleated. Estimate the material length required by working out the number and widths of pleats and add them to the width of the overlap.

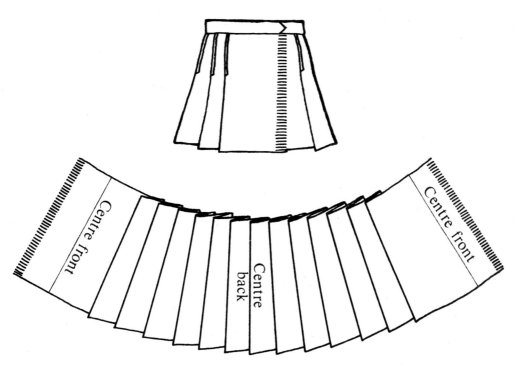

44 Kilt

This garment is very practical when made from
PVC which can be sponged clean easily. It is
suitable for young children and should not be
confused with the pinafore style which is a very
simple sleeveless dress.

Align the front bodice and skirt block along a
common centre front line with their centre waist
points touching. Put the hip points of the skirt
blocks together and close the waist to eliminate
the shaping at this point. If there are any darts
in the skirt blocks, put them into the hemline by
closing them at the waist. From the centre front
to the centre back mark off half of the waist
measurement. Draw the shape as shown in the
diagram, or something similar. The bib is held in
place by a strap round the neck and the back is
fastened by a tie or looped over a button. (This
would be easier for small children.)

The skirt section is constructed by one of the
previous methods and the bib, which is attached
to the skirt in the front, is based upon the bodice
block to achieve the correct proportions. (If the
skirt is plain it can be cut in one with the bodice.)
The skirt is joined to the waistband which fits
into the bib edge and is elasticated at the back to
give a secure fit. Allow for the width of the
waistband by taking a similar amount from the
bottom of the bodice block. The length of the
straps is calculated by placing the shoulder seams
of the bodice blocks together and measuring
from the bib over the shoulder to the back waistline. It is usual for the straps to cross at the back.
This prevents them slipping from the shoulders
as well as enabling them to be cut straight.

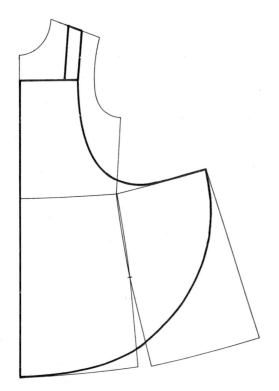

45 Apron

The bib is in two parts, a front and back section joined at the shoulder. The neck opening is made large enough to slip over the head and a zip or button fastening is inserted into the sideseam. An alternative version for a small child could consist of an elasticated waistband and open shoulders, fastened with buttons and buttonholes, which would also allow for adjustment in length.

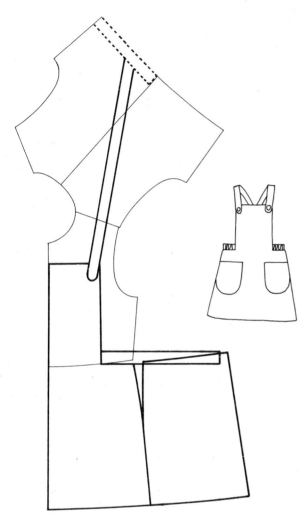

46   Skirt with bib

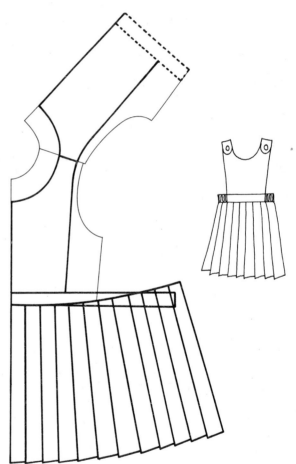

47   Skirt with bib-variation

Back

Trace round the skirt block leaving sufficient room to the right of the centre back for the extension. This should be slightly more than the measurement C–D.

On the centre back mark off A–B and A–C.

Square C to D and bisect the angle B–C–D to establish C–E.

Connect B–E–D with a good curve to form the crotch shape.

From D square a line to meet the extended hemline and complete the crotch section of the culotte.

Front

Repeat the instructions for the back except for drafting the extension to the left of the centre front. Measurements C–D and C–E are different from those of the back.

SIZE	92	98	104	110	116	122	128	134	140	146	
A–B	10·5	11	12	12·5	13·5	14	15	15·5	16·5	17	*Waist/hip length*
A–C	18	19	20	21	22	23	24·5	25·5	27	28	*Body rise plus ease*
C–D	9·0	9·4	9·8	10·2	10·6	11	11·4	11·9	12·4	12·9	*Back*
C–E	3·2	3·4	3·6	3·8	4·0	4·2	4·4	4·6	4·8	5·0	
C–D	5·0	5·2	5·4	5·6	5·8	6·0	6·2	6·5	6·8	7·1	*Front*
C–E	3·0	3·1	3·2	3·3	3·4	3·5	3·6	3·7	3·8	3·9	

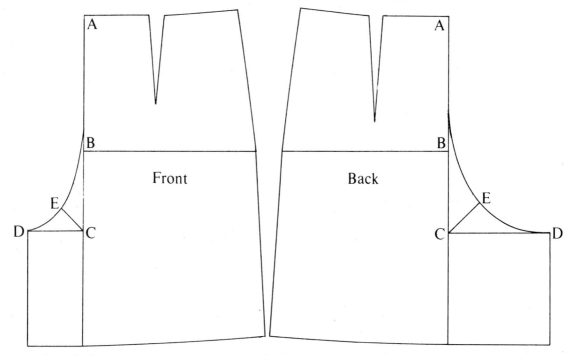

48a   Culotte draft

Diagram 48b
To insert the pleat cut along the centre front and
centre back lines to separate the crotch sections.
Move these sections out the required amount,
about 6–10 cm, to establish the width of the pleat
as shown. Complete the draft by adding turnings
and balance marks.

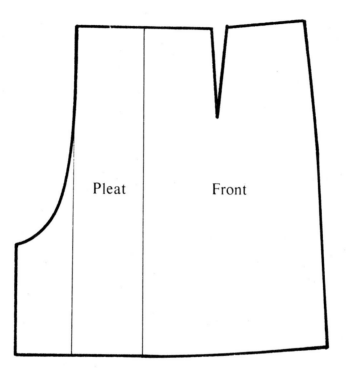

Pleat   Front

48b   Inserting pleat

Section 7   Collars and hoods

COLLARS

No one part of a garment should be considered separately from the whole, but quite often the collar assumes considerable importance. It is in a very prominent position on any garment and is subjected to intensive consideration by designers and pattern cutters.

It is important to identify and understand the parts of the collar which form the whole. Two main areas which affect the appearance and fit of a collar on a garment are the neck edge and the outside edge. If the shape of the neck edge is exactly the same as that of the garment neckline, the collar will lie perfectly flat but, as the neck edge curve straightens out, the outside edge will get correspondingly shorter, causing the collar to develop a roll along its length. This roll is known as the fold line and is the natural division between the outside of the collar, which becomes the fall, and the inside of the collar, known as the stand. It is the interplay and change between these parts, plus the styling of the outer edge, which allows such variety in collar styling.

Diagrams 49a, b, c and d

These illustrations show how the appearance of a simple shaped, flat collar (a) alters as the outside edge of the collar is shortened. This is achieved by slashing from the outside edge to the inner neck edge and overlapping the outer edge to shorten it. The neck edge becomes less curved and a fold line appears to define the fall and stand which

become more noticeable as a semi-roll collar (b) or a full-roll collar (c). In the final illustration, the neck edge is perfectly straight with the collar standing up (d). This is the effect the collar will have if the neckline remains closed. Some collars, however, are made to be convertible so

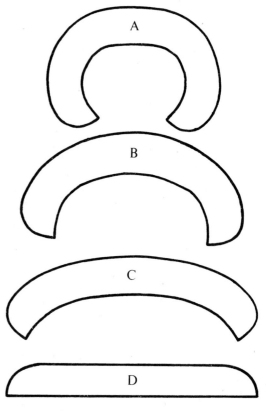

49a–d   Development of a flat collar

that the neckline can be opened. In these cases a collar will become flatter in appearance because the controlled length of the outside edge will be released, causing the collar to spread.

Although the range of collar styles is so wide that it is impractical to mention more than a few, they do fall into recognizable types. The styles given here are those which will be of greatest use for children's patterns. The drafting instructions are generally for one half of the collar. To make a full pattern, place the centre back of the completed half collar to a fold of pattern paper.

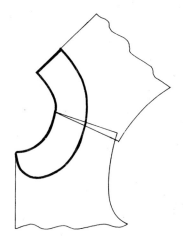

50   Peter Pan collar

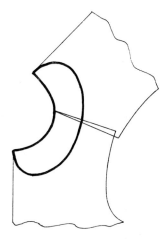

51   Two-piece Peter Pan collar

This is the simplest type of collar from a constructional angle, but is capable of great styling variety. One of the most popular of children's collar styles, the 'Peter Pan' is representative of this style. This can be cut as a one-piece collar if it is on a garment with a centre front opening, or as a two-piece collar if there is a centre back opening.

Diagram 50   Peter Pan
Place the shoulder seams of the basic bodice blocks together at the neck point and overlap them 1 cm at the armhole. This is the first step for all flat collars, with slightly less of an overlap for the smaller sizes. Trace the neck edge smoothing out the corner which might appear at the neck point and from here measure the width of the collar an equal distance all round. As a guide, the width could be approximately half the length of the shoulder seam. Round the corners at the front and put in balance marks at the centre back and the shoulder seam points. The overlapping of the shoulder seam causes a very slight roll at the back of the collar and should not be confused with roll-collar types. It is so constructed to minimize the chances of the neck seam (where the collar is attached to the garment) rolling up and looking unsightly.

Diagram 51   Two-piece Peter Pan
Repeat exactly as for the Peter Pan, except that the collar corners are rounded at the centre back as well as the centre front.

Diagram 52   Sailor collar
Align the bodice blocks together for a flat collar. Lower the neckline, on the centre front line, to the chestline. This depth is of course dependent entirely on the effect required. Connect this point smoothly to the neckline with a straight line running it in at an appropriate point.

Draw the style line of the outer edge of the collar. Trace the collar shape onto pattern paper or card, putting in balance marks at the centre back and shoulder seam points.

Diagram 53   Puritan collar
This is basically a very wide Peter Pan collar being at least as wide as the shoulder. Construct exactly as for a Peter Pan collar adding the extra width.

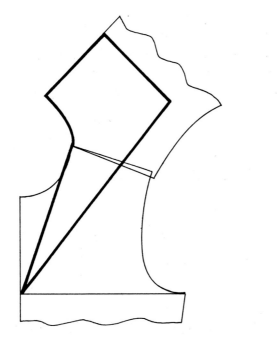
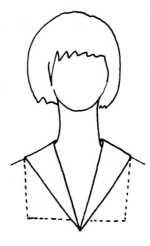

52   Sailor collar

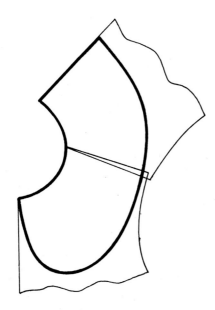
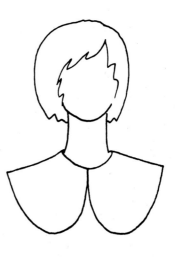

53   Puritan collar

As the name suggests, this collar type is midway between a flat and a full-roll collar. The stand should be appreciably less than the fall. The Eton collar is the most widely known of this type.

Eton collar   Diagram 54

Place the bodice blocks together at the neck point and pivot so that they overlap 3 cm (slightly more for the larger sizes) at the shoulder. Trace round the neck edge and straighten the V-shaped area which occurs at the neck point. As this new line can be slightly shorter than the original, add any extra length needed for the neck edge to the centre front.

From the new neckline edge, measure out the required width of the collar. This should be approximately two-thirds of the shoulder length.

Add 1·5 cm to the centre back width and re-draw the outside edge from this point, connecting the line smoothly to the front of the collar as shown in the diagram. This allows for the depth of the collar stand and enables the fall of the collar to remain the same width all the way round.

As the neckline has been altered, check that the shoulder seam balance point is in the correct position when placing in the balance marks.

This construction produces the basic sit and roll of the collar, but the design of the collar at the outer edge is of course variable.

ROLL COLLARS

The collar tends to flatten towards the front neck. In its most extreme form the full collar roll is sometimes known as a Turtle neck – merely a straight strip rolling over equally all round. In practice, however, this is not satisfactory unless it is cut on the bias, without a seam at the outside edge, enabling the collar edge to stretch slightly over the neckline seam. Also, to create a complete Turtle neck effect the fastening needs to extend through the collar, which can be bulky and impractical.

The commonest form for a roll collar is for the stand and fall at the centre back to be almost equal. This is where the greatest degree of roll occurs and it fits closely to the neck. At the front neck, the collar tends to flatten if there is a centre front opening.

Roll collar   Diagram 55a

Trace round the front bodice block and extend the shoulder seam line at the neck point. Using this as a guideline, place the back neck point to the front neck point, A, and trace round the neck area. Extend the back neck line from A through the centre front neck point.

Measure from the centre back neck to a new centre front point, B, to form the neck edge of the collar. This length is the neckline measurement of the block.

Draw in the style line required, remembering that the width at the centre back will be reduced by half to allow for the depth of the stand.

Put in balance marks.

Diagram 55b

If the depth of the collar stand is too narrow and does not create sufficient roll, slash into the neck-line at its most curved area, and dart to reduce the length of the outside edge.

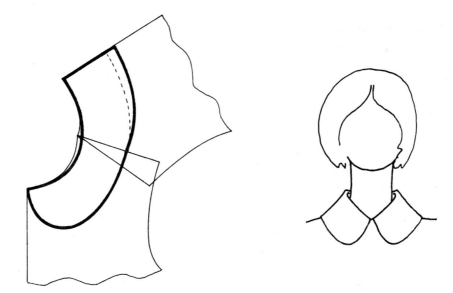

54   Eton collar

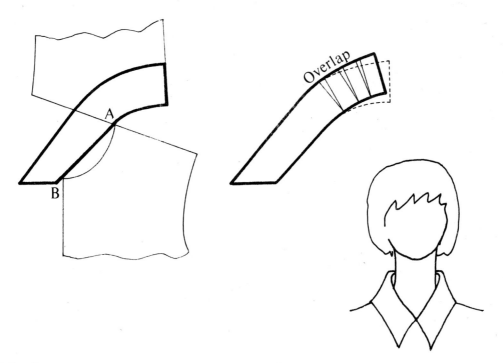

55a   Roll collar

55b   Shortening the outer edge

MANDARIN OR MILITARY COLLAR

This is a plain stand up collar and in its simplest form can be a straight band. However, a better fit is achieved if the front is slightly shaped.

Diagram 56
Cut a rectangle to the following measurements:

A–B equals half the neck measurement.

A–C equals half the back neck length.

A–D equals the required collar width.

From the top edge slash towards the neck edge to a point three-quarters of the distance between B–C.

Overlap the slashes so that point B is raised about 1 cm.

Smooth the top line, shape the front edges if needed, and trace off putting in a balance point at C.

SHIRT COLLARS

There are two styles which are important: the convertible collar and the classic shirt collar.

The convertible collar   Diagrams 57a and b
As its name suggests, this can be worn open or closed. It meets at the centre front neck of a garment and is often used for girls' sporty blouses and shirts. The draft is very simple.

Diagram 57a
Cut a rectangle to the following measurements:

A–B equals half of the neck length.

A–C equals half of the back neck length.

A–D equals the required stand depth. As a guide, Size 92: 2·0 cm, Size 146: 3·0 cm.

A–E equals twice the stand depth plus 1 cm. From the top edge, slash towards the neck edge to a point three-quarters of the distance between B–C. Overlap the slashes so that point B is raised 1·5 cm.

B–F. This is the style line which is variable.

F–E. Connect these points with a curved line to form the outside collar edge. Trace off the collar

shape marking a balance point at C.

Diagram 57b
If the outside edge is too tight, make a couple of slashes in the shoulder area and spread them open to allow more ease along the outer edge.

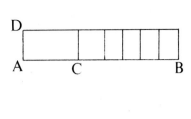

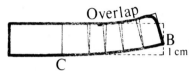

56   Mandarin collar

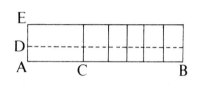

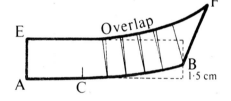

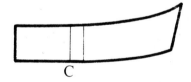

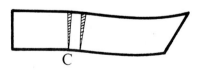

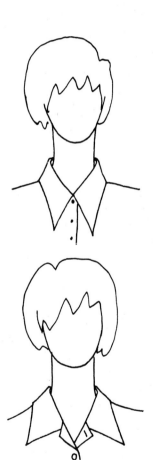

57a   Convertible collar
57b   Spreading the convertible collar

Classic shirt collar   Diagrams 58a and b
This is the collar generally found in mens' and boys'
shirts. It can have a separate or all-in-one stand.
The built-in stand differs from the convertible
type in that the stand is extended beyond the centre
front point to the full width of the wrap. The fall
of the collar does not extend beyond the centre
front because this would cause the front edges to
overlap.

Diagram 58a
Draft a rectangle from the following measurements:
   A–B equals half the neck length.
   A–C equals half of the back neck length.
   A–D equals the stand depth. This can be deeper
than a convertible collar stand. From the top edge,
slash towards the neck edge to a point three-
quarters of the distance between B–C. Overlap
the slashes so that point B is raised 0·5 cm to B1.
   B1–E. The width of the wrap extended from
B1. Connect E to the original top edge of the
rectangle at F with a curved line. This is the collar
step.
   F. This is the point at which the centre front
line from B1 crosses the original top edge of the
stand. Trace off the stand along lines A–C–B1–
E–F–D, placing balance marks at B1–C–F.
   To establish the outer collar, trace round the
collar stand. Extend the centre back line at A
by 0·5 cm to allow for the collar roll. From the
centre front point at F, draw in the outer collar
style line connecting it to A, and cut out. In the
shoulder area, slash from the outer edge to the
inner edge as shown. Spread each slash open,
about 0·3 cm, to make the collar spring slightly
away from the stand. Trace off the outer collar.

Diagram 58b
For the all-in-one collar, do not slash open the
outer collar when it has been cut out. Instead place
the two edges together and trace round.

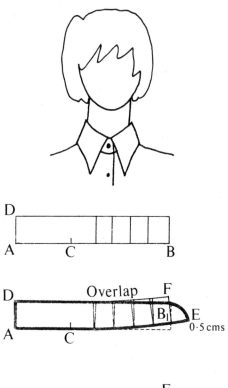

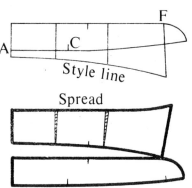

58a   Classic shirt collar with separate stand

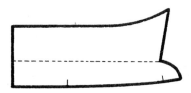

58b   Shirt collar with all-in-one stand

A revere is formed when the facing of the centre front opening is folded back as an integral part of the collar style. The collar is drafted so that the revere lies permanently in its correct position.

The draft for this collar is based upon proportions which give a neat simple shape for whatever size is constructed. It is essential that some of the basic measurements alter from size to size because, unlike adult blocks, the differences in measurement between the smallest and largest sized children's blocks is wide. The width of the wrap and depth of the neckline are appropriate for a classic collar draft, although most designers would only use this as a basis for their own ideas. For simplicity of explanation, the draft is based upon the basic bodice block, although in practice it might be the coat block. However, the principle is exactly the same.

Simple revere collar   Diagram 59
Trace round the basic bodice block and establish the width of the wrap parallel to the centre front. Establish the break point, A, on the edge of the wrap and the correct distance down from the chest line. Extend the shoulder line and measure B–C. Connect A–C and extend the line beyond C to E, forming the basic foldline. C–E is half the back neck length plus the C–E measurement in the chart. Where the foldline crosses the front neckline, mark point D.

SIZE	92	98	104	110	116	122	128	134	140	146	
WRAP	1·5	1·6	1·7	1·8	1·9	2·0	2·1	2·2	2·3	2·4	*Wrap width*
A	2·0	2·1	2·2	2·3	2·4	2·5	2·6	2·7	2·8	2·9	*Below chest line*
B–C	1·5	1·6	1·7	1·8	1·9	2·0	2·1	2·2	2·3	2·4	
C–E	0·3	0·3	0·3	0·4	0·4	0·4	0·4	0·5	0·5	0·5	*Plus half back neck*
F–E	1·0	1·1	1·1	1·2	1·2	1·3	1·3	1·4	1·4	1·5	
G–F	2·2	2·3	2·4	2·5	2·6	2·7	2·8	2·9	3·0	3·1	
H–G	5·0	5·2	5·4	5·6	5·8	6·0	6·2	6·4	6·6	6·8	

F–E. Square from E. Connect F–D to form a new fold line.

G–F. Square from F to establish the stand depth. Connect G smoothly into the front neckline to form the neck edge of the collar.

H–G. Square from G. This is the back width of the collar which includes an allowance for the foldline.

Measure the neck edge length of the collar, D–G, and check this against the equivalent neck edge on the bodice section. Adjust at G if necessary.

Connect D to I on the edge of the wrap through J which is the centre neck point.

At J construct a 45° angle. J–K equals J–I.

Connect K–H, and using this as a guideline, draw in the finished shape of the collar edge with a smooth curved line.

Run the line into the centre back of the collar, at a right angle inside H, to eliminate any point which could be formed in this area. Curve the line at the front part of the collar to help reduce any drag on the bodice at this point by narrowing the width of the collar. (If, when the collar has been proved in calico, it still drags, slash from the collar edge up to point D and open up about 0·5 cm to lengthen the outside edge of the collar.)

Clearly indicate balance points at D and at a point on the neck edge of the collar opposite the shoulder seam, before finally tracing off the finished collar shape with the tracing wheel.

Double-breasted revere collar   Diagram 60
Follow the instructions given for a single breasted collar, except for the different measurements in the chart below.

One general guideline which can be followed is 'the wider the wrap, the lower the break point'. If the break point on a double breasted style is too high, the basic fold line will cross over at too high a point and would cause discomfort at the base of the throat.

The diagram illustrates how the depth of the breakline in conjunction with a wider wrap alters the whole set of the collar at the centre back.

This causes the neck measurement from point G to shorten. To compensate for this, the allowance added to measurement C–E is slightly more for a double-breasted style. The revere collar is variable depending upon what effect is required. A simple way of establishing any style is to draw the correct shape on the bodice (the dotted line) and then fold the line D–A so that the shape of the revere can be traced off with a tracing wheel. The front part of the collar may be drafted at the same time.

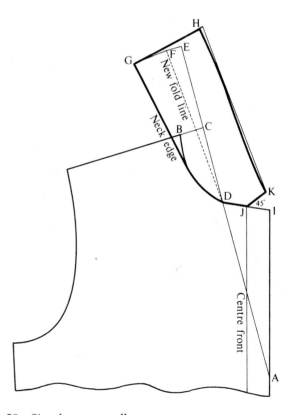

59   Simple revere collar

80

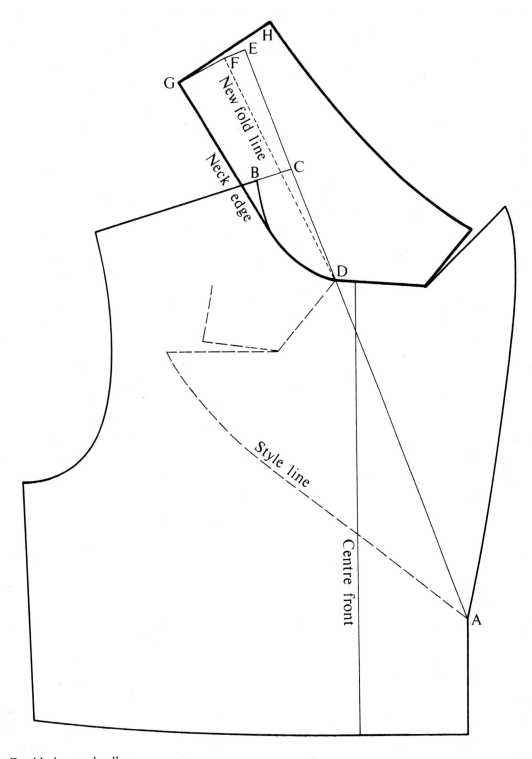

Labels within figure: H, E, F, G, New fold line, Neck edge, B, C, D, Style line, Centre front, A

60 Double-breasted collar

SIZE	92	98	104	110	116	122	128	134	140	146	
WIDTH	5	5·2	5·4	5·6	5·8	6·0	6·2	6·4	6·6	6·8	*width of wrap*

A midway between chest and waist lines.

| C–E | 0·5 | 0·5 | 0·5 | 0·6 | 0·6 | 0·7 | 0·7 | 0·7 | 0·7 | 0·7 | *plus half back neck* |

TOP AND BOTTOM COLLAR PATTERNS

Unless a collar has a perfectly straight outer edge, enabling it to be cut on a fold, it is usual to have top and bottom collar patterns. If they were cut from the same pattern the top collar would cause the seam edge to roll over towards the outside and look unsightly.

When a collar has been drafted, it becomes the under collar. For the top collar, trace round the under collar and add two to three millimetres extra width on the outside edges. Run this line smoothly into the centre front neck point, keeping the neck edges of both top and bottom collars the same.

HOODS

These can be separate, or attached, the second being perhaps most useful and practical method for children because unlike other forms of head-wear the hood cannot be lost. Any draft of a hood must be extremely basic because one of the important measurements, the neck edge, depends entirely on the length of the garment neckline. For this reason the draft must be treated purely as a guide. The amount of shaping taken out in the form of seams and darts to achieve the required fit will be a matter of personal judgement.

Basic hood   Diagram 61

Construct a rectangle to the appropriate width and length, marking in points A, B, C and D as shown.

Extend B–E and connect D–E.

In its crudest form, by gathering D–E into the neckline, this shape could now be used as a simple hood. It is better to give it more style by reducing the neck edge through darting or easing, and by shaping the lines A–C–D.

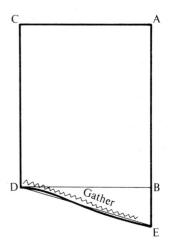

61   Basic hood

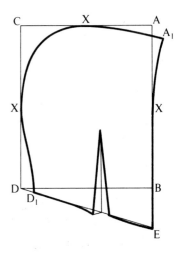

62   Round hood

82

SIZE	92	98	104	110	116	122	128	134	140	146
WIDTH	20	20·2	20·5	20·7	21	21·2	21·5	21·7	22	22·2
LENGTH	24	24·3	24·6	24·9	25·2	25·4	25·7	26	26·4	26·7
B–E	6·0	6·1	6·1	6·2	6·2	6·3	6·4	6·5	6·6	6·7

Round hood   Diagram 62

Construct a rectangular basic hood and make points X midway between A–B, A–C and C–D.

Point A1 is 2 cm below A, and 1·5 cm to the right of line A–B.

Point D1 is 2 cm from D along the line D–E.

To eliminate the excessive fullness in the neck edge, it is necessary to make a dart. The placement and width of the dart will depend on how much fullness needs to be removed. If possible, align the dart with the shoulder seam, distributing any surplus fullness evenly either side of the dart. Make the dart between 9 and 12 cm long by erecting a line from D1–E to cross the line D–B at right angles. Fold the dart out and connect to D1 with a curved line. Connect D1–X–X–A1–X with a good shape, as illustrated, to complete the back seam.

Round hood variation 1   Diagram 63

This variation takes away some of the fullness from the crown of the head by inserting darts at this point. Follow the instructions for the round hood, up to and including the drafting of the dart, then complete the following:

C–F is one-third the length of C–A.

C–H is one-third the length of C–F.

Square lines out from points F to meet at G.

Connect points H to G.

H–I is one-third the length of H–G.

Square guide lines from points I to the edge of the rectangle.

Connect D1–X–I–G–I–X–A1 with a good shape to complete the back seam and form the dart.

Round hood variation 2   Diagram 64

This style has a squared effect across the top of the crown. Complete the instructions for the previous method up to the establishment of point G. There is no need to position point A1. Connect D1–X–F–G–F–A. When making a hood from this pattern, it is usual to put line F–A to a fold. Points F go together to make the seam line across the top of the head.

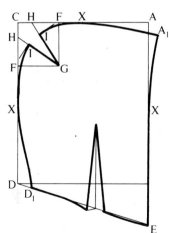

63   Round hood variation 1

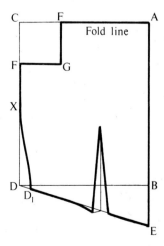

64   Round hood variation 2

83

Section 8　　Capes

Capes were originally cut very short, just covering the upper part of the body. They could also be part of another garment, such as a cloak, and were added to give extra protection across the shoulder area. This purpose is no longer necessary and nowadays a cape is generally accepted independently as a sleeveless form of outerwear. As such it can be fitted and tailored or full and very dramatic. The length is variable and many different styles can be evolved from three basic types. These are the circular, semi-circular and fitted capes.

BASIC BLOCK ALTERATION　DIAGRAM 65

For cape styles, it is necessary to make a slight alteration to the block so that a level hem can easily be constructed. Instead of the underarm points, the shoulder points are made level. As the back shoulder is higher than the front, the alteration is made to the back block. Place the blocks so that the centre front and centre back are parallel and the shoulder points are level with each other. Re-draw the back under-arm line at right angles to the centre back and level with the front under-arm line.

As the length of the cape increases, the fullness or sweep of the hem increases accordingly. This can result in large pattern pieces, so to contain pattern pieces within fabric widths and avoid unnecessary wastage, the style must be carefully considered before drafting the pattern.

Although the diagrams are based upon the bodice block, the instructions can be used just as easily for the coat block as most of the measurements are proportional to measurements within the block. As the cape is normally an outer garment this could be more appropriate.

Semi-circular cape　Diagram 66
Mark in the under-arm line A–B on the front block and the new under-arm line C–D on the back block. Place the shoulder and the under-arm points together. Pivot the front block at the shoulder so that the distance between points B–C is half of measurement A–B. This is the minimum width and any less will cause the cape to pull over

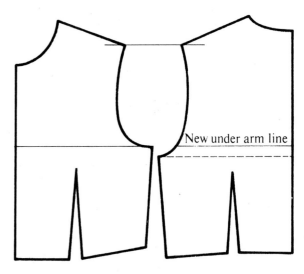

65　Basic block alteration

the upper arm. As the block is pivoted mark the path of point B to form a curved line. This is the broken line in the diagram. Connect B–C and make E–F the required back length. Make A–G equal to D–F. To establish the sideseam, bisect the shoulder angle and construct a line to cross the broken line at H and continue towards the hemline at I. Make H–I equal D–F. To construct the hemline, square lines out from points F, I and

G and use these lines to establish the shape of the hem as shown in the diagram.

It is usually necessary to have a sideseam because of fabric economy and style requirements. Without a sideseam, which is possible on smaller sizes if economy is unimportant, there is a dart at the shoulder. In both instances it is better to taper the shoulder seams to just below the shoulder points to eliminate possible poking in this area.

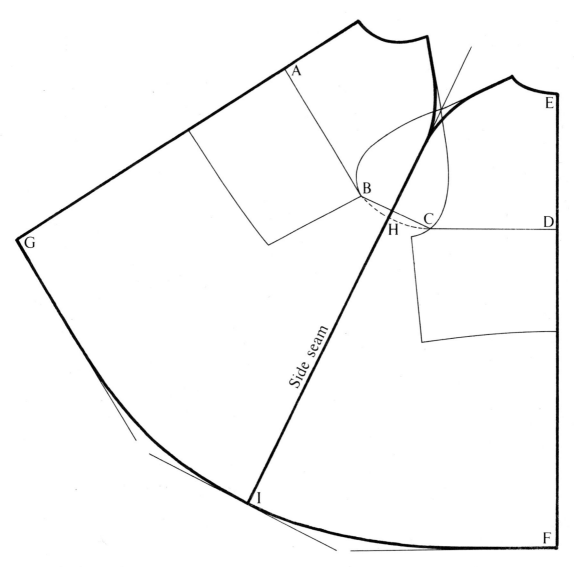

66 Semi–circular cape

Circular cape   Diagram 67

Place the centre back of the back bodice block to a straight line and put the shoulder and underarm points of both blocks together. Pivot the front block at the shoulder point so that the centre front is at right angles to the centre back. Mark the path of point B as shown by the broken line. Establish the sideseam and hemline in a similar manner to the semi-circular cape.

To make a fuller circular cape pivot the front block so that the shoulder dart is completely closed allowing the maximum amount of fullness to be drafted into the cape. This does result in very large pattern pieces, and could be very uneconomic in the use of fabric unless the cape is styled to produce smaller pattern sections.

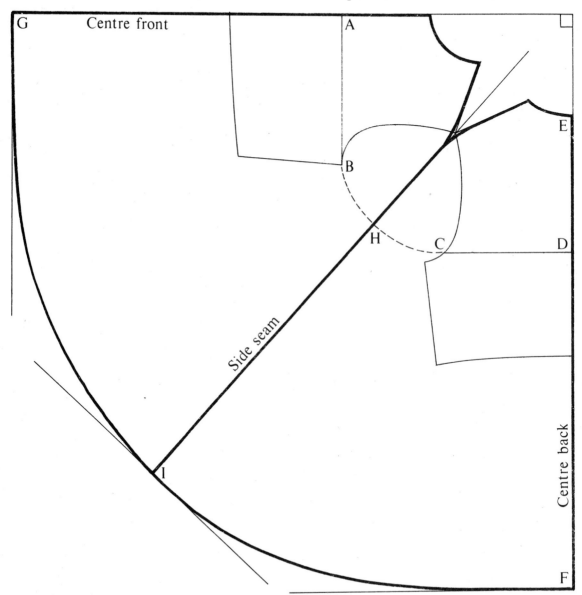

67   Circular cape

Fitted cape   Diagram 68

Mark the under-arm line A–B on the front block and the new under-arm line C–D on the back block. Align these lines on a common line, making the centre front and centre back parallel. The blocks are placed so that the distance between the under-arm points is approximately one and a half times the length of A–B.

Back

Extend D–C so that C_1 is directly above the original under-arm point. C_1–F is one-quarter of the original under-arm measurement. G–H is the cervical to knee measurement given in the following chart.

SIZE	92	98	104	110	116	122	128	134	140	146
G–H	51	54	57	61	65	69	72	76	80	84

H–I equals F–D plus one-third the length of F–D. Connect I–F extending the line beyond F to cross a line extended from the shoulder seam. Bisect the angle and measure out 2 cm to J. Connect F to the shoulder point with a curved line through J. Curve the hem up at the sideseam to avoid any sharp angle occurring.

Front

Extend A–B. B–E is one quarter of A–B. A–K equals D–H. K–L equals A–E plus one-third the length of A–E. Connect L–E extending the line beyond E to cross the line extended from the shoulder seam. Bisect the angle and measure out 2 cm to M. Connect E to the shoulder point with a curved line through M. Curve the hem up at the side seam the same amount as the back and dip it slightly in front to allow for the curve of the stomach. Put in balance points at appropriate places.

This style of cape can be attractive if the centre fronts meet edge to edge rather than overlap. Frog fastenings can be used, preferably above the waist level.

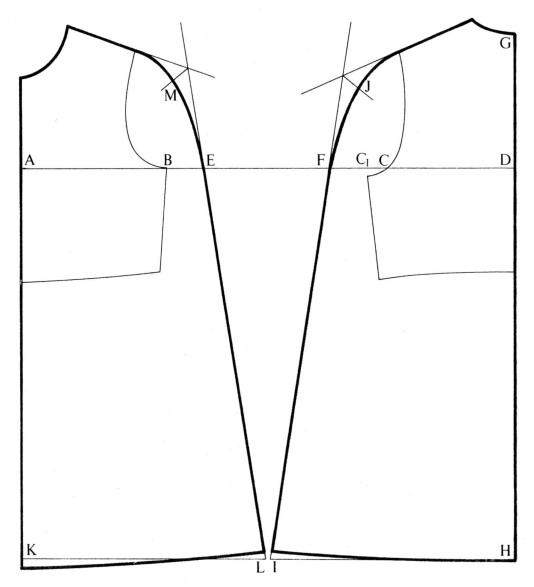

68   Fitted cape

Poncho Diagram 69
This garment, which originates in South America, is very easy to draft. Decide on the size by measuring from the back neck to where the point of the back corner of the poncho is required to hang (the cervical to knee length is a good guide). Construct two lines twice this length which bisect each other exactly at right angles. Connect the corners to form a square. Place the blocks on the same side of one diagonal with their neck points touching each other. Trace off the neck shape. Turn the blocks over and repeat the process so that the neck shape is completed. Make the neck opening, to whatever depth is required, on the centre front line.

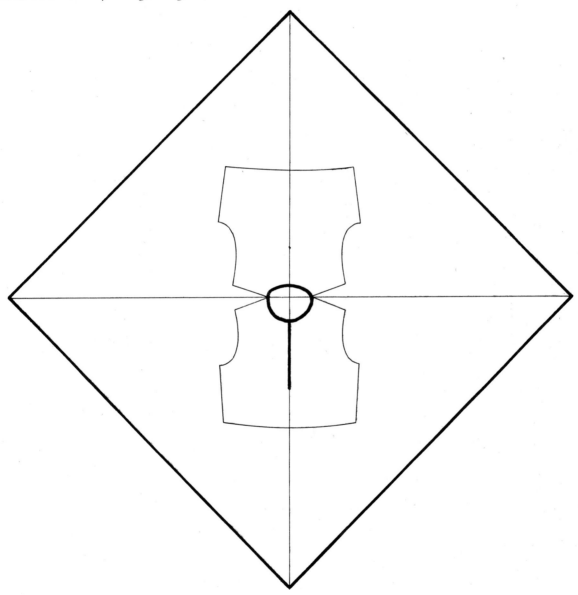

69   Poncho

Section 9   Designing children's clothes

The whole field of fashion design is constantly reflecting social and technological change, and therefore it cannot easily be subjected to any constant set of values, rules or regulations. Perhaps the nearest one can come to having any standard in fashion is that it must be right for its time no matter how ridiculous or tasteless it might appear in retrospect. These generalizations hold true for children's wear particularly now that adult fashions can be very quickly interpreted for children's styling.

Having made these brief statements I will now contradict them by suggesting some guidelines which can be considered when designing and pattern making for children. These are personal views and I would not presume that they express everyone's opinion about design, which is, after all, an extremely personal area of each person's awareness and appreciation of aesthetic values.

One of the first and most obvious considerations that should be remembered when designing children's clothes is that they are for *children,* and that the manner in which they treat their clothes is quite different from that of adults. They are unlikely to remain impeccably behaved every minute of the day or to keep spotlessly clean, particularly if they are boys or children of pre-school age. They will climb trees and crawl down holes, trudge through the only puddle in sight, sit on the floor instead of a chair, wipe sticky fingers down their clothes and explore the most unlikely and dirtiest places that they can find. In

their energetic and mobile everyday lives, their clothes receive far less care and attention than that given by adults to their own garments. The natural inquisitiveness of children will not change, and while I would not recommend designing an outfit for tree climbing, other than as an ergonomic exercise, it is necessary that clothes should take into account the nature of children's lives. It is essential to come to terms with the two major points which affect the design of these clothes: practicability and wearability. Both these qualities have been greatly helped by the tremendous technological strides that have been made by the textile industry. This has been in two main areas, the discovery of synthetic yarns such as acrylics and polyesters with their inherent easy-care properties, and the ability to inject these advantages into the more traditional fibres to achieve such things as drip-dry cottons and machine washable wool. Developments in knitted fabrics have meant that children's clothes do not have to look a couple of sizes too large to allow for growth, and perhaps justify the cost. With non-iron materials, permanent pressing and uncrushable fabrics it is possible to create for everyday wear exciting ideas in colour and fabric without losing sight of the principle aims – easy care for the parent and easy wear for the child. It is always possible to indulge in the more impractical fabrics for special occasion garments, party and bridesmaid dresses or fancy dress outfits.

DEVELOPING A BASIC STYLE

Simplicity of shape and cut with a minimum of fussy detailing should be one of the main objectives. The scale is so small, particularly on younger children, that the more a garment is divided into sections, the more complicated and unattractive it can become. The sequence of drawings in diagram 70 shows how the addition of only one style line on a simple dress, a yoke line, can be interpreted in various ways without losing the essential simplicity of the idea.

(a) Long sleeved simple dress.

(b) The front has been divided to form yoke and skirt sections. This enables the yoke to be in contrasting colours or materials.

(c) The skirt is gathered onto the yoke. The extra fullness is introduced into this section by slashing and spreading apart to insert the necessary width.

(d) The skirt fullness is introduced in another form – box pleats.

(e) The yoke has been changed to a V-shape to emphasize the inverted pleat in the skirt section.

(f) This is similar to the previous design except that the yoke has been split into two. This enables the striped fabric to form a chevron and introduce a further design feature which still blends with the whole.

These variations are quite straightforward and take no account of variations in sleeves, cuffs, pockets and trimmings, all of which can be a source of further ideas.

STYLE DETAILING

As part of the total look of a design, each element should be considered as part of the whole as well as being a satisfactory idea by itself. The proportion of a pocket, or something similar, should be exactly right to achieve the necessary affect and the shape should blend with the whole either in a contrasting or harmonious manner.

70a–c   Development of a basic style

Diagram 71 illustrates how the same basic design can be interpreted in different ways. Both dresses have the same simple shape, length of sleeve, depth of front opening, width of collar and two pockets. By altering the detailing on each style, a different effect is achieved. Design 71a is straight lined, crisp and angular, while 71b has a more feminine feeling introduced by curved detailing. In both designs collar, cuff tab and pocket detailings blend with each other in a logical manner.

Apart from altering details to create different design effects, there are also practical considerations to be observed. One of the major milestones in a young child's life is the ability to dress itself. This can be encouraged tremendously by having sensible fastenings and openings in its clothes. If possible, avoid back fastenings because children will have difficulty in doing them up. Make front openings deep enough so that garments can be stepped into, or have clothes button-through so that they can be put on like a shirt. Zips are easy, except for open-ended types which can be difficult to join for small inexperienced fingers. Cuff buttons are hard to fasten, so if no opening is needed for practical purposes it could be elasticated. Trousers for pre-school children generally have elasticated back waists and any fly opening effect on boys' trousers is normally decorative. If they are easy to hold, buttons present no great difficulty and toggles are also easy to fasten for a child. If a laced effect is needed, try to make it purely decorative and have the opening elsewhere. Young children find lacing difficult, especially if it is in an awkward position, and bows can easily become undone.

These are only guidelines and if it is essential for the look of a design that it has a back zip fastening or front laced opening then put one in. By concentrating on the practical considerations of a design it is often all too easy for the design to become boring and mundane.

70d–f   Development of a basic style

The most interesting development in fabrics during the past few years has been the emergence of knitted materials. They vary from sculptural double-knit jerseys to fine printed nylons and *Tricels* of much lighter weights. These materials with their built-in ease and stretchiness have helped to free children's design from being over concerned with enormous growth allowances. Clothes can look and fit better without losing this very important requirement.

There are really no fabrics which cannot be used for children's wear in some form although the choice of fabric for each particular design is most important. Apart from financial considerations, more expensive materials requiring a lot of care and attention would probably be best used on clothes which do not get a great deal of wear. For knock-about everyday clothes, tough, easy-care fabrics would be more important because of the tremendous wear they receive and the extra cleaning that is needed.

Be adventurous with fabric and colour. Do not have preconceived ideas that children only look good in nondescript, sensible shades. Colour is such an important feature in clothing that its choice and effect on a garment must be well considered, particularly when two or more colours or shades of one colour are being used. Clothes can be bright and cheerful in brilliant primary shades, pretty and feminine in soft pastels or rich and exciting in deep colours such as blacks, browns and purples. When designing, do not restrict yourself to ideas about colour and fabric which are generally thought to be safe and reliable. Put different colourways of the same pattern together or even different patterns, Gingham is an example of a material with which this can be tried. Mix spots and stripes with each other as well as with coordinated plain colours. Experiment with different textures to create contrasting surface interest, for example, fun-fur with corduroy or PVC with denim. Vary the surface of the fabric by quilting and padding, either selectively or all over. Try shirring the material or inserting piping cord, for a raised corded effect. Knit sleeves, collars or cuffs to contrast or tone with the main material. Fringe loosely woven fabrics. Use trimmings of all types, ribbons, braids, pompoms, appliqués, bows, buckles, and many others. Contrast a decorative zip to make it a feature of a design instead of toning it in. Try studs or frogging for fastenings, instead of zips and buttons. Contrasting top stitching and binding will add to the interest and potential of any design. Diagram 72 shows how one design can alter by using and applying various fabrics to the full, in this instance in the sleeve area.

(a) Simple dress with a bell sleeve.
(b) The sleeve is emphasized by a contrasting material.
(c) The bottom of the sleeve is braided and the braid is carried through as a tie detail.
(d) An entirely different fabric from the body of the dress is used for the sleeves, in this

71a and b Style alteration by detailing

case fun-fur with matching pom-pom
details.

(e) The sleeve is contrasted by cutting it on the
bias of the material.

CLOTH WIDTHS

Metrication affects the widths of various fabric
types as well as altering slightly the lengths in
which cloth is normally bought. At present,
there is a wide variety of cloth widths available
in Europe, and these appear to satisfy national
preferences as well as the suitability of a particular
yarn to a given width. In London, during the
autumn of 1971, the Fabric Buyers' Association
supported a proposal that industry should work
towards a standard 150 cm width for both woven
and knitted fabrics. Until this is implemented
throughout industry, fabrics will remain available
in a variety of widths. These will be basically 150
cm for suitings, knitted fabrics, and some dress
materials, and 100–115 cm for shirtings and other
dress fabrics. For the home dressmaker, materials
will be bought by the metre and tenths of a
metre.

PATTERN ALLOWANCES

Mention has been made many times throughout
this book about adding turnings and seam allowances to net patterns. These vary with different
parts of a pattern and also the type of material
being used. If a fabric has a tendency to fray, leave
a larger turning. With hemlines the general rule
is: the more curved a hemline becomes, the
narrower the depth of the hem. The allowances
should be treated as a guide, and where seams are
joined together it is normal for them to be the
same width.

0·5 cm   Necklines, sleeveless armholes, bag-
ging-out of non-fraying fabrics, e.g.
cuffs, collars, facings, pocket flaps etc.

72a–c   Designing around a basic sleeve shape

1·0 cm	As above for fraying fabrics, armholes and corresponding sleeveheads.
2·0 cm	Sideseams, shoulders, waistlines, centre back seams and narrow hems.
4–8 cm	Hem allowances, dependent upon possible alterations and the shape of the hem.

Although I have stressed the practical side of designing, do not become over anxious by the apparent impossibility of marrying exciting designs with practicality. Always consider any design idea, however strange it might appear, because without losing the essence of a design by subtly altering seamlines or the position of a fastening, it can usually be made to work in a feasible manner. It is important to remember that quite often good design can be the result of a solution to an essentially practical problem.

72d and e   Designing around a basic sleeve shape